The MLA~~~~~
of Documentation

A Pocket Guide

Michael Pringle
Gonzaga University

John Gonzales
Whatcom Community College

Prentice Hall
Boston   Columbus   Indianapolis   New York   San Francisco
Upper Saddle River   Amsterdam   Cape Town   Dubai   London   Madrid
Milan   Munich   Paris   Montreal   Toronto   Delhi   Mexico City
Sao Paulo   Sydney   Hong Kong   Seoul   Singapore   Taipei   Tokyo

VP/Editorial Director: Joe Opiela
Acquisitions Editor: Brad Potthoff
Assistant Editor: Jessica Kupetz
Editorial Assistant: Nancy C. Lee
Director of Marketing: Tim Stookesbury
Executive Marketing Manager: Megan
   Galvin-Fak
Senior Marketing Manager: Sandra McGuire
Marketing Assistant: Jean-Pierre Dufresne
Senior Managing Editor: Linda Behrens
Senior Operations Supervisor: Nick Sklitsis
Operations Specialist: Mary Ann Gloriande
Senior Art Director: Anne Nieglos

Cover Art Director: Jayne Conte
Cover Designer: Margaret Kenselaar
Manager, Cover Visual Research &
   Permissions: Karen Sanatar
Full-Service Project Management: Elm Street
   Publishing Services
Composition: Integra Software Services
   Pvt. Ltd.
Printer/Binder: Bind-Rite
Cover Printer: Lehigh-Phoenix Color
   Hagerstown
Text Font: [9/11 New Century Schlbk]

Credits and acknowledgments for material borrowed from other sources and reproduced, with permission, in this textbook appear on page 61.

Microsoft® and Windows® are registered trademarks of the Microsoft Corporation in the U.S.A. and other countries. Screen shots and icons reprinted with permission from the Microsoft Corporation. This book is not sponsored or endorsed by or affiliated with the Microsoft Corporation.

Library of Congress Cataloging-in-Publication Data

Pringle, Michael.
   The MLA style of documentation / Michael Pringle, John Gonzales.
      p. cm.
   Includes bibliographical references and index.
   ISBN 978-0-13-604973-9
1. Authorship–Style manuals.   2. Scholarly publishing–Handbooks, manuals, etc.   3. Academic writing–Handbooks, manuals, etc.   4. Bibliographical citations–Handbooks, manuals, etc.   I. Gonzales, John.   II. Modern Language Association of America.   III. Title.

PN147.P76 2009
808'.027–dc22

2009028541

10 9 8 7 6 5 4 3 2 1

Prentice Hall
is an imprint of

www.pearsonhighered.com

ISBN 10:   0-13-604973-7
ISBN 13: 978-0-13-604973-9

Contents

Preface

The MLA Style of Documentation: A Pocket Guide demonstrates the fundamentals of documentation for collegiate writing. It also offers a discussion of academic honesty, a sample student essay, and a helpful section on finding, evaluating, and integrating sources. It should prove sufficient for most undergraduate needs, and will remain a useful reference even for graduate students.

This guide is intended as a quick reference for citing accurately in the MLA format. It concentrates on the types of sources students are most likely to use, and while it covers a broad range, it is not comprehensive. The definitive guide remains the *MLA Handbook for Writers of Research Papers*. More advanced students considering submitting an essay for publication in a scholarly journal should refer to the *MLA Style Manual and Guide to Scholarly Publishing*.

This book has greatly benefited by attention from the editor and copyeditors. We would like to thank them for their expert assistance. We are also indebted to the reviewers who helped improve the guide by providing thoughtful and astute commentary. They are:

We thank our reviewers, whose many suggestions have greatly improved our text: James Allen, College of DuPage; Anne Balay, Indiana University Northwest; Rochelle Becker-Bernstein, St. Johns River Community College; A. Boumarate, Valencia Community College; Mark Coley, Tarrant County College; Gail S. Corso, Neumann College; Mark Crane, Utah Valley University; Michael Crum, Coastal Carolina Community College; Christopher J.L. Cunningham, University of Tennessee at Chattanooga; Jason Denman, Utica College; Bonnie Devet, College of Charleston; Michael W. Donaghe, Eastern New Mexico University; David B. Downing, Indiana University of Pennsylvania; Beverly D. Fatherree, Hinds Community College; Karen Gardiner, University of Alabama; Michael Hricik, Westmoreland County Community College; Holly Hunt, Metropolitan State College of Denver; JoAnne James, Pitt Community College; Jeff Kosse, Iowa Western Community College; Cynthia Kuhn, Metro State; Sally L. LeVan, Gannon University; Terry Mathias, Southeastern Illinois College; Susan Miller-Cochran, North Carolina State University; Emily H. Moorer, Hinds Community College; Diana Nystedt, Palo Alto College; Megan O'Neill, Stetson University; Trey Philpotts, Arkansas Tech University; Patti R. Smith, Jones County Jr. College; Victor Uszerowicz, Miami-Dade College; Sharon K. Walsh, Loyola University Chicago; Linda S. Weeks, Dyersburg State Community College; Cheryl A. Wilson, Indiana University of Pennsylvania; Cheryl Windham, Jones County Jr College; and Lynn Wollstadt, South Suburban College.

Introduction

This guide reflects the current standards set forth in the *MLA Style Manual and Guide to Scholarly Publishing*, third edition, 2008, which institutes significant format changes—many of them in response to developments in electronic technology and media. Readers conversant in Modern Language Association (MLA) style of the past will notice changes in several areas: MLA now encourages italics rather than underscore for titles, no longer requires URLs for most online sources, asks for both volume and issue numbers for all scholarly journals that have them, and calls for the labeling of the medium of publication or composition for all sources. If you are used to MLA style, then in-text citation will remain familiar, but we suggest that you refer to works cited examples in this guide until you are comfortable with the new changes.

So who uses MLA? The MLA style of citation is commonplace throughout the humanities, but it is not used exclusively in any particular field. It is a valid form of documentation in all cases, but various publications, disciplines, and teachers prefer and expect other types of citation—others include CMS (*Chicago Manual of Style*), APA (American Psychological Association), and the Number System. The standard for citing legal documents and court rulings is *The Blue Book: A Uniform System of Citation*. Find out which specific style of citation is required for your research-writing task before you begin.

There are two main components to MLA documentation: **in-text citations** to all referenced sources (whether direct or in parentheses) and a **Works Cited section** (the focus of the second half of this guide) to which they correspond. MLA documentation is meant to be as accessible, as useable, and as streamlined as possible for both the writer and the reader. When you cite your sources as a research writer, you demonstrate authority and support your ideas and your position, but more important, your documentation guides your readers to the sources you have gathered so that they might pursue further the concepts and issues introduced in your work. Furthermore, proper documentation allows you to enter into a scholarly conversation that ideally extends well beyond any single essay.

1

Plagiarism

Plagiarism is an *extremely* serious issue in the academic world because our educational system is committed to protecting ethics and integrity in the transmission of information. Freedom of information and inquiry comes with the obligation of academic honesty. Understanding what type of information must be cited and then properly documenting all your sources are the keys to avoiding plagiarism, and this manual is designed to assist you in correctly documenting sources in the MLA style.

Plagiarism at its most severe is a form of fraud or theft, and the plagiarist is viewed as a thief and a cheat in scholarly circles as well as in the publication industry. In some cases plagiarism breaks the law, but all forms of plagiarism constitute academic dishonesty and may subject a student to serious penalties. (Policies differ among institutions, and you should familiarize yourself with your school's.)

The general expectation throughout the scholarly community is that all sources of information—except for those that provide what can be regarded as **common knowledge** (see the expanded definition in the Key Terms list in Chapter 3), such as standard dictionaries or encyclopedias—must be acknowledged and cited. The variety of source matter that must be cited includes, but is not limited to, the original content of all forms of verbal text (including literary, nonfiction, and technical writing); creative expression, output, structure, and design; original arguments or analyses along with their results or conclusions; original illustrative and graphic materials; and independently derived research and research findings.

That's right: original words, images, and ideas are considered forms of creative and intellectual property, and they are protected by law as such.

Academic Honesty

Documentation styles such as MLA exist not simply to provide technical guidelines for academic research, but to help maintain the highest standards of academic honesty in all scholarly communications. All of us who write and present information within the academic world need to be clearly aware of the expectations and rules for integrating source material into our own writing and public presentations in order to uphold academic honesty.

Plagiarism has become increasingly easy in the era of word processing and the Internet, which make the inducement even greater for some to take shortcuts. Most instructors, however, are attuned to the methods and stratagems typical of plagiarism and immediately recognize the stylistic differences between a student's scholarship and a professional's; they are also quite aware of the major ideas, arguments, and research pertaining to their fields. Like you, they use and know how to navigate the Internet, and they are also aided by online plagiarism-detection services such as Turnitin.com, CheckForPlagiarism.net, and iThenticate.com. Sophistication in identifying plagiarism keeps pace with methods for accomplishing it. Don't be tempted!

Plagiarism negates any merit a student's paper or presentation may otherwise have had, damages irreparably the credibility of the perpetrator, limits the possibility of independent and critical thinking, diminishes the trust between teachers and students, and undermines the accomplishments of those who struggle and succeed through their own efforts. Plagiarism can and has resulted in severe legal consequences. Much as with instances of copyright infringement, the stakes can be extremely high when money is involved, resulting in multimillion-dollar lawsuits. Penalties for students who have succumbed to the temptation to plagiarize in their academic work tend to be more modest, of course, ranging from a failing grade to expulsion, but the results can be equally devastating for the offending party.

All the information you present in a scholarly context and do not cite is assumed to be your words and ideas. "Forgetting" to cite a source you've used is akin to forgetting to pay for something at the mall—explaining to your professor that it was just an accident is like trying to explain to mall security how an unpaid-for CD got in your pocket. Presenting others' words, key ideas, or research findings without appropriate and complete acknowledgment, whatever the circumstances, whatever the original intent, violates academic honesty. As we discussed previously, the only sources exempted from the need for documentation are the types of reference materials that maintain what is considered to be **common knowledge** (again, see Key Terms list in Chapter 3), such as standard dictionaries and encyclopedias. This may sound potentially confusing, but the easy rule of thumb is to cite all your source material unless it is clearly common knowledge.

Plagiarism Defined

Most definitions of plagiarism emphasize two aspects:

1. The **direct** act of knowingly presenting another's words, creativity, research, findings, or ideas as one's own in either exact or **paraphrased** form. In short,

plagiarism at its extreme involves falsely taking credit for someone else's thoughts and efforts.

2. Presenting others' words, key ideas, or research findings without appropriate and complete acknowledgment. Various types of **misattribution** might be a matter of error or oversight, but failing to set quotation marks around a directly quoted excerpt from another's work or omitting a correct citation, whatever the intent, still constitutes plagiarism.

Direct Plagiarism

Copying and pasting from one or several existing sources, purchasing a complete essay from an online plagiarism mill, or "borrowing" an essay from a friend, even with that friend's permission, are typical examples of this sort of plagiarism if you submit the results as your own work. This remains true whether it is a matter of an entire paper or just a few sentences. It remains true if you strategically intersperse plagiarized material with your own writing or if you combine and interweave a number of different sources without proper documentation. While these examples typically take the form of exact, **word-for-word** (**verbatim**) reproduction from a secondary source, such as might be readily found on the Web, **paraphrasing** (putting another author's thoughts and ideas into your own words) is also plagiarism if the original source is not clearly and directly acknowledged. Remember, too, that the unique, distinctive structure of a source is protected along with its original concepts and ideas.

Misattribution and Plagiarism

The second category of plagiarism, **misattribution**, may well occur without a writer's intending to deceive the reader or appropriate the work of another. An oversight in the mechanics of acknowledging a reference source or the inadvertent omission of an acknowledgment or a citation are examples of misattribution. While most instructors are aware that honest mistakes occur in documentation, the complete omission of a citation always casts doubts on the author's integrity. Further, giving incorrect information about one's source can be defined as plagiarism through misattribution as well—again, regardless of the intent! And finally, under "fair use" practices as they are outlined on Turnitin.com, "copying so many words or ideas from a source that it makes up the majority of your work, whether you give credit or not," is yet another form of plagiarism.

Academic honesty promotes individual critical thinking along with respect for and responsibility toward the work of others. Zero tolerance for plagiarism is a way of honoring students who work to attain these standards. And while this particular guide focuses on the MLA style of documentation for academic writing, it is important to realize that the strictures against plagiarism apply with equal force when you convey information through PowerPoint® or another media- or graphic-based presentation format, as well as in an oral delivery.

Examples of Plagiarism

The most blatant kind of plagiarism is carried out when a student "lifts" some portion of an existing work—often by copying directly from a Web-based source—and passes it off as her or his own. Direct plagiarism also occurs when exact words, ideas, and concepts are paraphrased (i.e., reworded but substantively identical), or even when a distinctive presentational structure is used without acknowledgment and under false pretense of ownership.

No matter how cleverly the concepts are reworked or reordered, if the author or source that originated them is not acknowledged, the result is still plagiarism. Nor does it matter whether or not the plagiarized source is of particularly high quality or prestigious authorship, as we demonstrate with the next example. Both word-for-word and paraphrased plagiarism are shown by integrating the introduction from a hypothetical student essay on *The Merchant of Venice* into a second student-authored source that is readily available on the Internet. The plagiarized sections are underlined for clear identification.

1. Original Source Material

Despite the fact that this is an obscure source written by a high school student, if it is used then it must be cited as surely as if it came from the venerable pages of *Shakespeare Quarterly*.

Karren, Max. "Dominant Themes in William Shakespeare's *Merchant of Venice*." *Helium*. n.d. Web. 6 Aug. 2008.

> *The Merchant of Venice* by William Shakespeare shows how the absence of mercy leads to the downfall of humankind. Initially this is shown through Antonio's hatred of Shylock the moneylender. Also, the play demonstrates how Shylock's lack of mercy leads to his demise. Lastly, Portia's hypocrisy ensues the final tragedy in *The Merchant of Venice*.
>
> In *The Merchant of Venice*, Antonio's hatred of Shylock and lack of understanding or sympathy triggers the line of unfortunate events to come. Antonio's heartbreaking role is foreshadowed in the opening act of the play. "I hold the world as the world, Gratiano; A stage where every man must play a part, and mine a sad one" (1.1.77-80). The relationship between Shylock and Antonio indicates their own character's demise as well as the failure of surrounding roles. Both of their religious beliefs preach kindness and good will, but their stubbornness attributes indifference for one another. This is evident when Shylock moralizes, "I hate him for he is a Christian," then continues, "Cursed be my tribe if I forgive him!" (1.3.48-49). In response to Shylock's ranting, once again Antonio uses his faith to crutch his lack of mercy, insisting, "The Devil can cite scripture for his purpose" (1.3.96). Antonio's contempt for Shylock floods the dike. It becomes the diffusion of chaos, and source of conflict for Shakespeare's *The Merchant of Venice*.

Word-for-Word Plagiarism

Mercy is a word repeated again and again in William Shakespeare's play *The Merchant of Venice*, and it is the single most important theme throughout. It applies to all of the play's main characters, and to all of us. In fact, <u>Shakespeare shows how the absence of mercy leads to the downfall of</u>

humankind. Initially this is shown through Antonio's hatred of Shylock the moneylender. It becomes the diffusion of chaos, and source of conflict for Shakespeare's *The Merchant of Venice*.

Plagiarism Through Paraphrase

Mercy is a word repeated again and again in William Shakespeare's play *The Merchant of Venice*, and it is the single most important theme throughout. It applies to all of the play's main characters, and to all of us. In fact, Shakespeare equates the absence of mercy to the overall collapse of humanity. He first demonstrates this through Antonio's contempt for Shylock's unmerciful lending practices, which eventually lead to Shylock losing everything. Their antagonistic relationship and mutual indifference reflects on other characters as well, especially Portia, whose hypocrisy brings about the tragic finale in the play.

And finally, here is a validly documented version, combining a direct quote and an appropriately cited paraphrase. Please note that this version not only cites the source matter, but, in contrast to the other two examples, it also poses an original concept that draws upon the source in a precise and limited way without simply restating its position.

Properly Cited Version

Mercy is a word repeated again and again in William Shakespeare's play *The Merchant of Venice*, and it is the single most important theme throughout. As Max Karren has noted, the absence of mercy is a crucial factor in the antagonism between Antonio and Shylock, and a central "source of conflict" for the play as a whole (1). Yet it is not a simple distinction between merciful and unmerciful attitudes that Shakespeare explores. It is the "quality of mercy," as the disguised Portia phrases it in the famous courtroom scene of Act IV, that is of most concern within the play. Shakespeare challenges his audience to consider, or even to reconsider, the quality of mercy as they understand it. So we must go beyond the notion proposed by Max Karren that there is a "failure of surrounding roles," to uphold mercy and instead reflect on mercy in a more absolute sense (1). The very religious, social, and interpersonal foundations of mercy are explored throughout the play. Portia, Antonio, and the Duke seem satisfied that they have rendered due mercy in response to Shylock's unmerciful demands; the audience, however, is left to contemplate the inconsistencies and contradictions inherent in the expression of mercy at all levels within this complex text.

Other kinds of direct plagiarism include the use of others' research findings or personal experiences without giving due credit. We can't emphasize this enough: it is vital to remember that plagiarism does not refer only to exact words; an author's unique conclusions, research, and style of presentation are all protected intellectual property as well! In some cases plagiarism breaks the law, but all of these forms of plagiarism constitute academic dishonesty and may subject a student to serious penalties. These final examples are drawn from the arena of statistical information as compiled and presented by a well-known professional author. They again demonstrate both **word-for-word** and **paraphrased** plagiarism—this time from a book by Jared Diamond—and again the plagiarized sections are underlined for clear identification. The plagiarized paraphrase is entirely stolen, despite the rewording.

2. Original Source Material

Diamond, Jared. *Collapse: How Societies Choose to Fail or Succeed.* New York: Viking Penguin, 2005. Print.

> In 1992, eight years after the state of Colorado had issued an operating permit to Galactic Resources, the company declared bankruptcy and closed the mine on less than a week's notice, leaving a large local tax bill unpaid, laying off its employees, stopping essential environmental maintenance, and abandoning the site. A few months later, after the start of the winter snowfalls, the heap-leach system overflowed, sterilizing an 18-mile stretch of the Alamosa River with cyanide. It was then discovered that the state of Colorado had required a financial guarantee of only $4,500,000 from Galactic Resources as a condition for issuing the permit, but that cleanup would cost $180,000,000. After the government had extracted another $28,000,000 as part of the bankruptcy settlement, taxpayers were left to pay $147,500,000 through the Environmental Protection Agency.

Word-for-Word Plagiarism

In 1992 Galactic Resources declared bankruptcy and closed their mine leaving a large local tax bill unpaid, and abandoning the site. A few months later the maintenance system overflowed, polluting an 18-mile stretch of the Alamosa River with cyanide. Colorado had required a financial guarantee of only $4,500,000 from Galactic Resources, but the cleanup would cost $180,000,000, of which taxpayers had to pay $147,500,000.

Plagiarism Through Paraphrase

Western states have not required sufficient financial guarantees for environmental cleanup from mining corporations. For example, the mining company Galactic Resources was required to guarantee only $4,500,000 for cleanup by the state of Colorado, but when they filed for bankruptcy the state was able to get back only about $28,000,000, leaving the Environmental Protection Agency with a bill of $147,500,000, which taxpayers had to fund.

Properly Cited Paraphrase and Word-for-Word Quotation

Jared Diamond argues that western states have not required sufficient financial guarantees for environmental cleanup from mining corporations. For example, the mining company Galactic Resources was required to guarantee only $4,500,000 for cleanup by the state of Colorado, but when they filed for bankruptcy the state was able to recoup only another $28,000,000, leaving taxpayers "to pay $147,500,000 through the Environmental Protection Agency" (457).

Our emphatic and pointed discussion of this topic is not intended to intimidate or frighten our student readers. Most teaching faculty do not relish the role of acting as plagiarism cops; most, in fact, find it the saddest of necessities. We recognize that the vast majority of students work extremely hard to achieve their educational success and to become accomplished, responsible, independent thinkers. Understanding what type of information must be cited and properly documenting all your sources are the keys to avoiding plagiarism, and this manual is designed to assist you in mastering the basics of the MLA documentation style.

2

Finding and Evaluating Sources

The Physical Library

For many generations of students, the campus library has afforded not only a quiet, comfortable place to study and undertake research, but also a special aura and atmosphere that lingers fondly in their memories when they recall their college days. In this "information age," however, many students would rather go online than go to the library—not an unreasonable preference with the constantly improving range and number of databases, online publications, and reliable Web sources available. Nonetheless, the physical library hasn't been rendered obsolete on the college campus just yet. Ignoring the print texts in your library, as well as the additional access to specialized and subscription databases a library provides, seriously limits the pool of nearby, reliable sources available to you. The operative term here is *reliable*. We now use the word "google" as a generic verb for conducting a Web search, but Google™ is a commercial vehicle, and it is designed with a commercial agenda. Although it seems like a no-brainer to say it, you will dramatically increase your effectiveness as a researcher by familiarizing yourself with your local library's physical resources, which include specific subject sections, documents, archives, and even the librarians themselves. Your online searches will also be enhanced by the increased access to scholarly databases you get by browsing through your library's search engine and by learning how to refine your searches and maximize their relevance to your needs.

The following is a list of library services with which you should be familiar.

Reference Librarian

One of the most valuable resources for a student learning to use the library is the reference librarian. A living, breathing professional who can answer most questions on the spot is something no electronic database can offer. Nonetheless, reference librarians are often very busy (even harried at certain times of the day), so the more focused and specific you can make your questions, the better. Many libraries offer free classes, organized and taught by librarians, on how to use the library. Others offer introductory tours on an individual basis. Check out the options at your library.

Library Catalog

Almost all American libraries now use computerized catalogs, yet this electronic resource is your essential guide to the print texts at your disposal. You can search by author and title of a work, but unless you already have a clear idea of what sources you need, subject or keyword searches may well be your best option. A subject search draws on the various Library of Congress subject headings that have also become the standard for classifying and organizing college library holdings. A keyword search can be a versatile tool, but, as with using a typical Internet search engine, patience and resourcefulness on your part may be necessary. The first terms you input will not always lead you to the best sources—you may get too many "hits," thus requiring you to narrow the search using more specific or fewer terms, which then requires the use of broader (or even different) terms. We recommend that you prepare a list of search terms in advance and that you plan to go to **the stacks** to examine potential texts to assess their relevance and usefulness for your project. The catalog provides a brief set of bibliographic details on each text along with its location in the form of a **call number**—carefully write this down!

Reference Section

This section, which is nearly always on the main floor of a library quite near circulation, houses a vast repository of encyclopedias, dictionaries, compiled facts, statistical data, bibliographies, lists, atlases, rankings, etc. Specific areas within the reference section are devoted to specific disciplines or categories, and it is worth your time to learn the reference holdings for your major as well as for the fields covered within your other course work.

The Stacks

The forest of bookshelves in a large library can be a bit intimidating, but they are arranged by subject, and only a few sections will be devoted to your discipline or current area of study. Learning the specific areas associated with your major can pay big dividends. Once you've found a few sources in the **library catalog** that match your topic, you can cruise the stacks in that region to see what else is there. This method can often turn up more appropriate sources than an extensive catalog search that may lack the most appropriate or compatible search terms.

Current Journals and Periodicals

Libraries generally subscribe to a variety of newspapers, popular magazines, and scholarly journals, the most recent of which they place on current-reading shelves or kiosks for a certain amount of time and then either store within the stacks or archive in some other way. Don't disregard this tremendously useful category of publications. Until a much greater percentage of reputable periodicals publish regularly online, bound periodical collections, particularly of **scholarly journals**, will remain among the most valuable resources available to the student researcher. Scholarly journals tend to be more current and digestible than the typical scholarly **monograph** (a book-length study), and, in fact, it is commonplace for a major scholarly concept or argument to see publication as a journal article before it reaches full elaboration in an independent volume. Many disciplines also combine articles on related topics within particular **issues**, and you will often find reviews of recent texts that have relevance to your own current investigation. While they lack the rigorous quality controls of their scholarly counterparts, other types of periodicals can also be beneficial sources owing to their immediacy and their capacity to reflect the world beyond academic circles. Because of the sheer physical bulk of so many periodicals in their original print medium, however, many libraries are shifting to electronic forms for storage. Another format for saving older periodicals is microfiche, which allows for far more compact storage but requires a special machine for reading it. It is definitely in your best interests to find out how your library stores the journals germane to your major or current research project.

Other Services

Modern college libraries often offer a wide range of services beyond housing and providing access to texts, such as writing labs, video collections and players, interlibrary loan options, group study space, copying centers, conference rooms—the list goes on and on, and it varies with each library. Find out what special services your library offers.

The Electronic Library

While virtually all college libraries have a collection of computer terminals dedicated to searching for information of all kinds, an even more convenient service many libraries offer is that of allowing you to browse through their search engines and databases from your personal computer. One helpful feature of remote access to online databases is the increasing availability of full-text documents, which you can locate and download from the comfort of your own home or dorm room.

The range of sources any library can hold has been increased exponentially by online databases, but most require paid subscriptions and are not available to you if you are not working through your library's search engine, typically accessed through the library's home page.

The variety of specialized databases available today can easily overwhelm and frustrate an unprepared student researcher; therefore, it is important to know the best databases to use when researching a given topic. Chances are your library will subscribe to some or all of the following databases. This selective list is useful for a general search through popular newspapers, magazines, multidisciplinary journals, government publications, encyclopedias, as well as online sources.

General Search

Academic Search Premier—a multidisciplinary academic database, some full text.

Article First—gives multidisciplinary journal article citations.

Books in Print—the best source for in-print, out-of-print, and forthcoming books.

GPO—Government Publication Index.

Ingenta—tables of contents for a wide range of journals.

JSTOR—offers full text for scholarly journals.

MasterFile Premier—many full-text, multidisciplinary offerings.

NationalNewspaper—a wide range of full-text American newspapers.

Newspaper Source—a wide range of full-text international newspapers.

ProQuest Direct—a range of interdisciplinary journals, some full text.

Topic Search—a current-events database.

Discipline-Specific Searches

Arts and Humanities (Selected Databases):

American History and Life—an index to American history articles in all eras.

Communication and Mass Media Complete—a major index for communication arts.

Contemporary Literary Criticism Select—contemporary literary criticism.

Dictionary of Literary Biography—biographical and critical essays.

Historical Abstracts—world history index from 1450 to the present.

MLA—Modern Language Association indexes (literature, language, linguistics, etc.).

Oxford English Dictionary—the most authoritative and complete English dictionary.

Philosopher's Index—a major index for philosophy students.

Religion and Philosophy Collection—an index for world religions and philosophy.

World History Abstracts—indexes and abstracts for world history.

Business and Law (Selected Databases):

ABI / INFORM Trade & Industry—a wide range of business-related indexes.

Business Source Premier—indexes of scholarly business journals.

EconLit—indexes for economic journals.
EDGAR—Securities and Exchange filings and information.
Find Law—directory of Web-based legal resources.
HeinOnline—a full-text collection of legal research material.
Industry Norms and Key Business Ratios—key business information.
Regional Business News—a full-text collection of U.S. business news.
Test Locator & Test Review—test and research information.

Education (Selected Databases):
eLibrary Elementary—a database aimed at the interests of K-6 students.
ERIC—a key educational resource, with citations and abstracts.
K-12—searches a range of databases for information geared to a young audience.
Mas Ultra—a database aimed at high school students' interests.
Professional Development—indexes to core educational journals.
SPORTDiscus—a full-text research tool for school athletics.
Test Locator & Test Review—test and research information.

Engineering and Applied Sciences (Selected Databases):
ACM Digital Library—Association of Computing Machinery online resources.
Agricola—indexes for agricultural literature.
Computer Source—full-text computer science articles.
Ei Engineering Village—Compendex Engineering Index and other indexes.
IEEE—full text of IEEE (Institute of Electrical and Electronics Engineers) journals.

Nursing and Medicine (Selected Databases):
Alt HealthWatch—coverage of alternative medicine sources.
CINAHL—Cumulative Index to Nursing and Allied Health.
Clinical Pharmacology—up-to-date pharmacology sources.
Health Source: Nursing/Academic—full-text scholarly journals.
ICN Union List of Journals—index to health sciences journals.
Medline—health sciences database sponsored by the National Library of Medicine.
PubMed—accesses Medline and other biomedical sources.
PubMed Central—a subset of full-text articles from the PubMed database.
Stat!Ref—full-text health-care reference resources.

Sciences (Selected Databases):
ACS Publications—full-text American Chemical Society publications.
Agricola—indexes for agricultural literature.
CRC Handbook—handbook of chemistry and physics.
Ebsco Animals—information related to biology.
Institute of Physics—online access to *Journal of Physics*.
MathSciNet—access to mathematical reviews.
PROLA—*Physical Review* online.
SciFinder Scholar—chemical abstracts online.
SPORTDiscus—a full-text research tool for school athletics.

Social and Behavioral Sciences (Selected Databases):
APA—American Psychological Association.
CIAO—Columbia International Affairs Online, political science sources.
Communication and Mass Media Complete—a major index for communication studies.
CQ Weekly—current congressional issues.
CultureGrams—cultural and sociological information.
National Criminal Justice Reference Service Abstracts—an index to criminology sources.
PsychiatryOnline—an important resource from the American Psychiatric Association.
PsychInfo—a vast archive of citations published by the APA.
Psychology and Behavioral Sciences Collection—indexes to psychology and behavioral topics of concern within the field.
Social Services Abstracts—indexes and abstracts for social science journals.
SocINDEX—a full-text social sciences index.
SPORTDiscus—a full-text research tool for school athletics.

Other Sources

A great many of the sources held in libraries and databases are **secondary sources** (with literary works being a large exception), but primary sources acquired through your own efforts and ingenuity can also be quite valuable. Interviews, lab research, unpublished diaries, and self-conducted surveys (to list only a few examples) can all add a great deal to a research paper. For example, if you have a relative who is an administrator at a hospital, and you find yourself researching the current shortage of qualified nurses, interviewing that person could add an authoritative, specifically focused voice to your position or argument. Be creative in your research, and consider all your available resources.

Evaluating Print Sources

A full discussion of research methodology is beyond the scope of this text, but the following is a basic guide to rating potential source material. Finding source material, often way more than you can use, is fairly easy for most subjects. Determining which sources are the most appropriate and reliable for your project may be a bit more difficult. This can be the greatest challenge—but for many, also the greatest reward—involved with a scholarly endeavor. A common pitfall confronting the inexperienced or overeager researcher is the impulse to grab the first few appropriate looking and easily available sources from the first page of a long list. Time constraints will often be a limiting factor in your research, restricting you to readily available choices (such as full-text online sources, holdings in your library, etc.). If you begin early and plan ahead, however, you can gain access to a far wider range of source material. Leave yourself time to sort through the likely prospects to determine which are most suitable for your project and to gather more difficult-to-get sources by other means, such as requesting a source through interlibrary loan, spooling through microfiche, conducting firsthand primary research (fieldwork), or even going to other local libraries.

Our discussion of source evaluation will focus predominantly on secondary rather than primary sources. A brief refresher: a **primary source** is an item of direct, immediate evidence; a **secondary source** is an analysis or interpretation in response to primary matter. A useful illustration of this distinction might be drawn from archaeology, where cultural artifacts comprise much of the primary source matter. The fact of the arti*fact*—a shard of pottery, an inscription in a tomb, a ceremonial mask—is its existence; the archaeologist's job (once authenticity has been established) is to place the artifact within a context in order to interpret and reach conclusions about its function, meaning, or significance, the written results of which would be developed and circulated as a secondary source. MLA users deal mostly with secondary sources, and they must determine what secondary sources will best enable them to conduct their own scholarly act of interpretation and analysis. When it comes to secondary sources, not all are created equally, and the fact of their existence does not automatically establish their validity or reliability.

MLA requires whenever possible a citation for each source that includes at least author, title, publisher, and date of publication. These vital statistics aid readers in locating the cited sources for themselves, but they also comprise the factors a scholar considers when determining the merits of a potential source. An easy-to-remember evaluative strategy is to subject a potential secondary source to the four C's: **credibility, collegiality, currency,** and **context**.

Evaluating by Author

The **author** profile is the single most important determinant of the viability of a scholarly source—therefore, be sure to scrutinize potential authors according to the four C's. What level of **credibility** does each author have? What credentials and expertise has he or she established within the relevant field of study? Consider such things as educational background, professional assignments and affiliations, publications or achievements in the field, and even awards or honors. Don't be wowed by titles alone: they can be misleading. A cardiovascular surgeon who decides to write about the Civil War may not have the historiographic knowledge and skills to do so in a credible manner despite having earned the right to be referred to as a doctor in the world of medicine. Particularly if the author is not a professional scholar, consider also the apparent purpose of the source. Let's face it: books by political candidates released at the height of a closely contested campaign have an intent other than the objective sharing of information. Corporate authors too should be critically assessed. A long-standing and prestigious organization such as the NAACP has more automatic and immediate credibility than the recently incorporated AntiAging Institute, even though both have undeniable agendas.

In offering the term **collegiality**, we encourage you to consider the extent to which the source and its author are situated within a larger dialogue among experts in that area. How completely does your author ground her argument and investigation on a variety of diverse and interesting sources generated by colleagues and peers? What is the range and abundance of sources the author cites? An author who offers little but an individual perspective, no matter how qualified an expert she might be, will likely be of less value to your project than an author who provides you a comprehensive familiarity with a broad spectrum of research and an expertise on a particular topic or issue. How completely has your author shown currency through an awareness of recent and ongoing research, and what new, compelling data is made available within the source? How recently was the source published? Has its content been superseded or severely contested by more current work? Finally, what is the context for the source—that is, under what circumstances and in what environment was the source generated, and within what framework do you hope to use it? Context may overlap with the first three C's, but in some situations, considering context might help you to see a valid use for a source that you might otherwise be inclined to disregard. For example, a source written in 1980 might initially seem to lack the **currency** you need for your essay on steroid use among today's athletes, but because of the **context** in which it was written, it could help to illustrate the relationship between social awareness and usage, an avenue you hadn't thought to explore.

A Helpful Suggestion: Scholarly sources thoroughly document their own extensive sources of information, so locating even one scholarly that source fits your project can provide a cornucopia of other valuable resources. So why not start there?

Evaluating by Publisher

A source's **publisher** is also an important indicator of reliability, and some publishers definitely have more **credibility** than others. As an extreme example from the category of periodicals, an article appearing in the *Economist* about the possible effects of speculators on oil prices would have a much higher level of reliability than a speculative article in *The Star* on the existence of Bigfoot (believe it or not, Bigfoot is a subject of academic study) despite the fact that both are newspaper opinion pieces. The most reliable sources in a specific field frequently come from academic presses and journals. Major organizations such as the American Psychological Association (APA), the American Chemical Society (ACS), and the Modern Language Association (MLA) generally publish the leading journal in their respective fields, and they also provide indexes to scholarly journals. **Scholarly journals** are very carefully edited for verifiable content, proper attribution and use of sources, and quality of contribution to the fields they cover. They contain articles by professionals and experts whose status and reputations rely on their credibility. Since they are generally **peer reviewed**, which means that other experts read and critique all submissions before they are accepted or rejected, these journals are exceptionally **collegial** by their very nature. This high level of professionalism in article selection and editing makes scholarly journals among the most reliable secondary sources. Though they seldom match the **currency** of journalistic periodicals and many Web publications (they are often published quarterly or even less frequently) scholarly journals tend to demonstrate that instant gratification can be at odds with reliability and that **context** can trump currency. Seldom will you see a leading scholarly journal forced to print a retraction owing to an error in reporting or an ill-considered or sensational statement. These journals nevertheless achieve an immediacy and currency far greater than **monographs** and classroom textbooks while maintaining a comparable degree of scholarly integrity.

Most books from successful publishers undergo extensive editing, but monographs from academic presses (usually designated as "University Press" on the title page) also undergo peer review and tend to represent the work of authors with high credibility and well-established expertise. A scholarly monograph can never match the currency of a scholarly journal because the quality-control measures for monographs take commensurately longer for longer works (and because, in honesty, the wheels of academic publication can turn slowly), yet their greater scale and scope allow for even more extensive collegiality.

In the arena of book publishing, texts released by independent **educational presses** stand next in the hierarchy of reliability. You may already be familiar with some major names: Pearson Prentice-Hall, Norton, Viking Penguin, Longman, and Bedford/St. Martin's are among the heavy hitters in the industry. These publishers, who produce texts mainly for student use, share a close relationship with the academic world, a relationship that demands a high level of credibility in their publications. Their quality-control standards are accordingly more rigorous than those of their trade or mass-market counterparts. Many prospective publications from educational presses undergo a process of peer review and subsequent revision to help ensure standards of both credibility and collegiality, which, again, impact currency. Trade publishers, on the other hand, whose products are mostly what you see filling the shelves, tables, and displays of any mainstream bookstore, have vastly different target audiences and standards different from those of publishers with an academic orientation. Their goal is to sell books in the greatest possible quantities, and aside from protecting themselves from culpability in plagiarism, they tend to circulate texts under the credo of *caveat emptor*, "buyer beware." Trade publications require neither collegiality nor often credibility in authorship, and despite the fact that they frequently exceed academic and educational publications in terms of currency, that seeming advantage is not so great that it should be a decisive factor in your choice. There are without question useful, credible sources available through trade publishers, but the onus falls more completely on the reader to scrutinize the author and the style in which the text is presented.

Evaluating by Date

The **date** of publication is important, but it is more critical in some disciplines than in others. A critical examination of Emily Dickinson's poetry from the 1960s might still be quite relevant, while a computer science text from the same time period would be woefully behind the times, perhaps even laughable, because of the technological advances in the field. Questions of **context** run parallel for both forms of scholarly media, particularly in light of the fact that the typical monograph has seen portions of its study published in article form within a scholarly journal while being completed.

A Helpful Reminder: If you are in doubt about the merits of a particular source, consult your reference librarian or, if appropriate, your instructor. Don't disregard your human resources in your quest for textual sources.

Evaluating Online Sources

Who publishes, or sponsors, a **Web site** is as important as who publishes or sponsors print sources, and often can be determined from the **domain name** when not indicated elsewhere. Most professional organizations have Web sites helpful for finding good online and print sources, and it is well worth visiting the sites most pertinent to your field of study. The Internet was originated not by Al Gore, but by scientists seeking a vehicle for regular and open communication, and that spirit lives on in many ways. Web postings allow for an accessible immediacy not possible with any other public medium; their **currency** can be in real time in some instances. The Web offers a wealth of uncensored, free, and open information that persists despite efforts to commercialize or regulate its flow, and the technology of hypertextual links allows for an extreme degree of **collegiality**. For all their abundance, variety, immediacy, and accessibility, however, online sources can present special problems because—to understate the case—many are not as carefully edited and reviewed as are their print counterparts. Anybody can put any opinion he or she wants on a Web site and can even post misinformation intentionally. The democratization of information thus doesn't automatically equate to increased reliability. Another difficulty online sources present is that the Web is constantly changing: a site that is accessible today may be gone tomorrow, or it may have been updated without warning to a newer version. Sometimes a source can exist online in several states of "update" at one time. Nonetheless, more and more great online sources are appearing every day, and the Web is fast becoming an essential venue for all disciplines.

One way to begin to evaluate an online source is to take a close look at its **Uniform Resource Locator (URL)**. This is the "address" that appears when you access a Web site, and it contains valuable information for determining the source's reliability, most notably in the **domain name** and **extension**.

http://www.americanheart.org/presenter.jhtml?identifier=3053

| Protocol | Domain Name | Extension | Document Path | File name/Identifier |

Protocol

The protocol tells the browser software what method of data transfer to use to access the information on that particular site. The abbreviation "http" stands for "hypertext transfer protocol," "https" for "hypertext transfer protocol secure," and "ftp" for "file transfer protocol." The symbols "://" separate the protocol from the domain name.

Domain Name

Technically, the domain name simply identifies the name of the server where the source material resides, but it is often the address for an organization's home page, and it will sometimes identify a corporate author as the source when no author is listed. For example, the URL listed above will take you to a page titled "Heart Attack/Stroke Warning Signs," which has no listed author. The American Heart Association can be assigned as the author of this article because the article is part of the list of links the Association claims as its own on its home page, and that attribution also appears in the URL. The home page also provides links to other sites (and therefore to other authors), which are clearly labeled both in the link and in the new URL. As with print sources, establishing authorship is crucial to gauging **credibility**.

Domain Extension

The domain extension can be very useful when you are scanning for reliable sites because it indicates the general purpose of the site host, the equivalent of the publisher in this medium. For example, ".org" and ".edu" extensions are reserved for nonprofit and educational institutions, respectively. While such designations do not guarantee the quality of a source, these sites are Web havens for reliable authors and institutions, and they will be most likely to offer the benefits of scholarly collegiality. Likewise, the extensions ".gov" and ".mil" designate government and military sites, and they carry the nominative reliability of the respective agency responsible for the site. Sites with ".com" or ".biz" extensions are business enterprises that may be more interested in advertising a particular product than in providing reliable information. The ".net" designation is generally for private use.

Document Path and File Name or Identifier

The last portion of the URL leads to the desired document and file, and it is case sensitive (meaning you have to be careful with capitalization). It is easier to cut and paste a long URL than to retype it. If you need to cite a URL and the document path portion is very long, it is best to cite the domain home page URL rather than reproduce an overlong identifier.

Citing Sources in Academic Writing

Key Terms

Block Quote   A **direct quote** that is longer than four standard lines of your regular writing. Such a long quote is set off from the rest of the work by indenting the entire quote ten spaces, or two indents. A block quotation has different **concluding punctuation** than regular direct quotes. See page 22.

Citation   A specific reference to a source that has produced a particular quote, concept, creative work, argument, statistic, analysis, or graphic material integrated into or referred to in a scholarly work; or, the process of systematically creating such references. Citations are forms of acknowledgment or attribution.

Common Knowledge

1. Information considered throughout the academic world to be of a factual nature and so generally agreed upon as to belong to the realm of what "everybody knows" (or perhaps what everybody should know), such as would be presented without qualification in a standard dictionary or encyclopedia: for example, that a noun is a naming word for living beings, places, objects, and actions; that the earth is in orbit around the sun; that Thomas Alva Edison developed the first viable incandescent light bulb. By contrast, specialized and rarely presented facts, such as the heart rate of an African crown eagle or the favorite book of Abraham Lincoln, should be attributed to a particular source of information. Because it is generally known and accepted, common knowledge will

appear in numerous sources and will essentially be taken for granted; thus it requires no citation or attribution in most instances as long as you state it in your *own words*.

2. A well-known quote or saying (proverb), such as "beauty is in the eye of the beholder" or "love is blind." Many of the phrases in this category are considered clichés, however, and should appear in your writing rarely, only when they most aptly express what the situation calls for.

Concluding Punctuation Punctuation that concludes a sentence can be a period (.), a question mark (?), or an exclamation point (!). As a general rule, concluding punctuation for a sentence comes *after* the parenthetical citation (not the end of the quote): (Author Page #). You should, however, keep an exclamation point or question mark that ends a direct quote at the end of the quote: "Lord, what fools these mortals be!" (3.2.115). The rules for punctuating block quotes differ slightly as well (see page 21).

Direct Quote An exact, word-for-word (verbatim) excerpt from another's work set off by quotation marks ("quote") or in block quote format in your writing. Be careful to quote accurately and fairly (in the proper context).

Documentation The **scholarly** process of carefully acknowledging your sources. The MLA style attempts to keep source citations streamlined in the main body of your text through parenthetical citations and to have each **in-text citation** correspond clearly to a full description of the **source** in the **works cited** section.

In-text Citation A brief reference to a source that will be more fully described in your **works cited** section. The MLA style of **documentation** employs parentheses around the particular source information that is not part of your running text. The examples throughout chapter 3 show a variety of ways to accomplish this.

Paraphrase To put source's words, ideas, research, or conclusions into your own words. This is a completely valid way of presenting another **source** in your work, as long as you cite the original source and are careful to represent it accurately.

Parenthetical Citation The MLA's economical system for labeling sources, primarily through author name and page number placed in parentheses. Parenthetical citations are used for both quoted and paraphrased material that is *directly* used in support of or as evidence within the body of the written text (as opposed to a consulted work or source that is never specifically referenced). See the range of examples in the following section.

Scholarship The research-based activities and products associated with professionals and students who participate in the broader academic conversation. Scholarly writing uses accepted documentation styles to acknowledge and credit its sources of information and to guide readers clearly and quickly toward those sources.

Source An informational resource; any text, Web site, artwork, chart, map, report, lecture, or interview that contributes to a scholarly project. Sources provide evidence, support, background, and authority. Sources are typically divided into two categories: primary and secondary.

primary source—a direct item of evidence pertaining to the subject under discussion; or, in the case of literary and artistic criticism, the actual text being critiqued. Other examples of primary sources include information from an experiment you conducted, data from a survey you administered, and (in most cases) a historical document you retrieved from an archive.

secondary source—external, after-the-fact commentary, research, or analysis relevant to your topic and particular position. Secondary sources will generally make up the bulk of sources undergraduates are asked to use, as they provide access to the expertise of professionals in any given field and allow you to benefit from the sum total of previous research in the area. For example, in an essay about class distinctions in *Twelfth Night*, Shakespeare's play would be a primary source, as would commentary on class issues by one of his contemporaries or a woodcut bearing a scene illustrating the concept. By contrast, a modern article by Anne Barton on the subject would be a secondary source. When you write a research paper for a college course, you add a secondary source to the pool of resources available in the world of information.

Summary   As a kind of comprehensive **paraphrase**, a summary condenses another author's main points into an overview or synopsis. As with paraphrase, it is important to carefully and accurately represent the original **source**.

Works Cited   In MLA format, an alphabetical list at the end of your work that corresponds to each **in-text citation** within your text and gives a full description of the **source**: author(s), title(s), editor(s), translator(s), edition, publishing data, dates, and medium (print, Web, photograph, etc.). The second half of this guide deals with the many variables of creating a proper works cited section.

In-text Citations and the Three Rules of Form and Format

Why Document Sources Parenthetically?

You could get around the necessity of parenthetical citation and a works cited section altogether if you incorporated complete source information into your own text at all points, but this would tend to be awkward and cumbersome (as well as be unacceptable in most academic venues). Compare the two citations below. The first uses parenthetical citation while the second resorts to full in-text documentation:

Diamond claims that a "suitable starting point from which to compare historical developments on the different continents is around 11,000 B.C." (35).

Jared Diamond claims on page 35 of *Guns, Germs, and Steel: The Fates of Human Societies*, published by W. W. Norton and Company of New York, in 1999, in print, that a "suitable starting point from which to compare historical developments on the different continents is around 11,000 B.C."

MLA parenthetical in-text citation streamlines source citation for the writer and the reader. The primary goal of in-text citation is to direct your readers quickly to the pertinent source in your works cited section and then, as precisely as possible, to the immediate point in the source from which the excerpt or paraphrase was drawn. A typical citation will consist of the author's last name and a page number (or a span of page numbers), separated by a space but no punctuation. A standard parenthetical citation in the text of your paper should refer your reader to the full bibliographic citation listed alphabetically in your works cited section. For example, if in your essay you **paraphrased** from the book by Jared Diamond listed below, the parenthetical **in-text citation** would look like this:

> Important divergences between human societies became significant beginning about 11,000 BC (Diamond 35).

Every in-text citation should lead the reader to a **works cited** reference, and a list of such references will make up the last page(s) of your essay, where all your sources will be listed alphabetically. Take a moment to look over the sample essay on pages 35–40 to see how in-text citations work in conjunction with the works cited page. Here is how the full works cited entry for the Diamond reference would be listed:

> Diamond, Jared. *Guns, Germs, and Steel: The Fates of Human Societies.* New York: Norton, 1999. Print.

Again, MLA style strives to be concise; here are three basic rules that will determine the form of your in-text citations.

1. Citing a Single Source by One Author

If you state the author's name in your text and use only a single source by that author, only the page number need be included in your parenthetical citation. Note that all directly quoted material appears in quotation marks ("quote") or **block quotes** to separate the author's words from your own. Be careful to integrate quotes grammatically.

2. Citing Multiple Sources by One Author

When you use multiple sources by the same author, your parenthetical citations need to include a title reference between author name and page number. You are allowed to shorten the title to one or two key words. The title is separated from the author's name by a comma. If, for example, your essay incorporates references to Edgar Allan Poe's "The Black Cat" and "The Fall of the House of Usher," a parenthetical citation differentiating "Usher" from "Black Cat" could adopt any one of the following forms:

> The narrator's own tendency to interrogate the validity of human perceptions throws into doubt the reality of what transpires within the narrative (Poe, "Usher" 231).

> Poe uses the narrator as a vehicle for expressing his own extreme doubts about the validity of "the shadowy fancies" that often comprise human perceptions ("Usher" 231).

Poe's "The Fall of the House of Usher" begins as an open interrogation into the nature of human perception, casting severe doubt on its validity (231).

The more you list in the parenthetical citation, the less you need to mention in your writing, and vice versa.

3. Punctuating and Formatting Citations

Incorporating and punctuating citations can vary according to the situation. **Concluding punctuation** for **paraphrase** and **summary** comes after the citation:

Bierhorst speculates that the relative isolation of South America and its unique flora and fauna have contributed to the mistaken notion that its mythology too stands apart from that of the rest of the world (14).

When **directly quoted matter** is integrated into your own text, quotation marks close prior to the parenthetical citation, while concluding punctuation for the sentence still comes after:

Though the wildlife and people of South America have developed in extreme isolation from other parts of the world, Bierhorst contends that "the general features of mythology, and even some fine points, are of world occurrence" (14-15).

Note: You'll notice hyphenated page numbers in this example; this is because part of the reference draws on ideas expressed on page 14 and the specific quote comes on page 15.

Block Quotes and Embedded Quotes

Block quotes are directly quoted excerpts of more than four standard lines, which must be set apart from your own text by indenting the entire quote ten spaces or one inch from the left margin of your writing, (generally, two "Tab" spaces). Block quotes are normally double-spaced, but you may match the spacing of your paper. You do not use quotation marks to enclose a block quote: Instead, it is the exceptional case where the parenthetical citation "floats" one space after the concluding punctuation:

With the exception of Australia, South America is the most isolated of the continents. More so than with North America, its plant and animal life and its human cultures have developed independently of the rest of the world. Accordingly, its myths . . . appear to have a life all their own. . . . On close inspection, however, South American myths turn out to be not quite so odd after all. (Bierhorst 14)

On two occasions, the block quote above uses ellipses (. . .) to indicate that some material within the quote has been omitted for the sake of economy. Please note that correct grammar and coherence are still preserved. In the following block quote, the author has inserted his own word, "by," in brackets, to keep grammatical sense.

Even though a block quote is set off by indentation rather than quotation marks, there may be quotation marks within the quote if your source cites another text. A quote within a quote is called an **embedded quote**, and it is formatted as follows:

> The *Mayflower's* passengers were, according to Bradford, "not a little joyful." The clarity of the atmosphere on a crisp autumn day in New England shrinks the distances and accentuates the colors, and the Pilgrims were "much comforted...[by] seeing so goodly a land, and wooded to the brink of the sea." Just to make certain, Jones tacked the *Mayflower* and stood in for shore. After an hour or so, all agreed this was indeed Cape Cod. (Philbrick 35)

To cite an **embedded quote** incorporated into your own writing, use the following format and punctuation:

> Philbrick details the difficulties of the Atlantic crossing and notes that the "*Mayflower's* passengers were, according to Bradford, 'not a little joyful'" (35).

Integrating Sources

Once you've found reliable and pertinent sources, you must integrate the information into your writing. Avoid quoting too much, and think in terms of how a source contributes to your thesis. Use block quotes sparingly, and only when a briefer excerpt is insufficient to illustrate or support your point. Remember that your voice should always direct your essay: if source material makes your argument for you, then it really isn't your argument. You may reference an idea, a direct textual excerpt, a series of pages, a chapter or chapters, or even an entire work in a single citation; however, writing well obligates you to preserve the clarity and continuity of your sources and to remain faithful to the context of the original work. Be careful to quote accurately and never to omit material to make a quote better fit your argument if the omission distorts or misrepresents the original. How the references contribute to the goal of the essay determines the extent to which any source should be used and therefore the scope of any given citation. The following examples show a range of ways to cite various types sources in your writing.

Citing Works by One Author

The most common type of citation requires only an author name (and page number when appropriate). It is the writer's obligation to incorporate quoted matter in a grammatically sound way. This may entail making slight changes to the quoted passage in terms of capitalization or punctuation. Such editorial changes are indicated by square brackets: [ ]. In the direct quote from Holm (right), the capital letter "T" is emended to a lowercase "[t]" to integrate the quote grammatically.

Direct Quote

Bill Holm notes that "[t]he more highly abstracted the design becomes, that is, the more nearly the represented creature, by distortion and rearrangement of parts, fills the given space, the more difficult it becomes to interpret the symbol accurately" (9).

Paraphrase

Interestingly, difficulties in interpreting Northwest iconography emerge not only when a symbolic figure is fragmented for lack of space, but also when it is expanded to fill space (Holm 9).

Two or More Works by One Author

A title—which can be shortened to key words—must be included in each citation where there could be confusion. For example, the full title of Ray Bradbury's novel listed below is *Something Wicked This Way Comes*. In MLA style, long works or single-volume titles are indicated by *italicizing*; titles of short works (such as poems, short stories, or articles that may be collected in anthologies) are placed in quotation marks.

... (Bradbury, *Something Wicked* 77).... (Bradbury, "Foghorn" 42).

Works with Multiple Authors

A citation for a work by two or three authors must list them all sequentially as they appear on the publication's title page:

Because film remains primarily a visual art form, some purists insist that "its golden age was the era of silent films" (DeNitto and Herman 50).

The famous *Federalist* opens with a plea for both "philanthropy" and "patriotism" on the part of its readers (Madison, Hamilton, and Jay 87).

Again, multiple authors must be listed in the order they are presented in the referenced source, which is not necessarily alphabetical. Citations for works by four or more authors need include only the name of the first listed author followed by the Latin abbreviation "et al." (which means "and others"), without additional internal punctuation. For example, the book *Habits of the Heart* has four authors, with Robert Bellah listed first, and may be cited as follows:

... (Bellah et al. 19).

Works with Volume and Page Numbers

If your works cited page includes entries for more than one volume of a multivolume work, your citations should include the volume number after the author name and introduce the page number with a colon, followed by one space and the specific page number.

... (Emerson 3: 211).

Corporate Author

Citations for works by corporate authors follow the same general rules outlined so far. If you have previously identified the group name by its abbreviation, subsequent citations can include it in the same fashion.

> The Science Fiction Research Association (SFRA) concedes that defining the genre is a tricky and uncertain proposition (ix).

> The fact that science fiction cannot be easily reduced or pinned down does not mean that it lacks categorical coherence or a clear literary history (SFRA xiii).

Note: Roman numerals are a common way to distinguish introductory and prefatory sections from the central text and should always be used within the citation.

Works with No Listed Author (Anonymous)

Apart from anonymously written literary classics, you should show a healthy skepticism of publications for which no one is willing to take credit. Online sources will sometimes present special difficulties in determining a specific author. Remember that corporations and institutions can also be authors, and that Web sites may have reliable editors or compilers even when no author is listed. If you opt to use a source with no author named, treat the title as the author and follow previous rules. As with other in-text citation titles, the full title can be abbreviated to a key word.

> . . . (*Beowulf* 45).

An anonymous online example is handled similarly, but remember that page numbers are rare for hypertext composed specifically for electronic media. When clear and practical, paragraph (abbreviated "par." or "pars.") numbers are a helpful guide for your readers. Note that this example replaces author name with a shortened version of the full title:

> People don't always think only of themselves in times of crisis. One man, for example, had gone out in search of the family cat. Meanwhile, the storm arrived, and "so changed the landscape he got lost" ("Happy Ending" pars. 4-7).

When there are no page numbers or paragraph numbers, you must cite the source in its entirety.

An Entire Work

If your reference pertains to an entire work rather than a specific passage, segment, or section, your citation needs to indicate only the author's name, either within the written text or in a parenthetical citation. Many Web sources have no page or paragraph numbers and therefore must be cited as entire works.

> Norris' work exemplifies a "naturalist aesthetic" (Campbell).

The full works cited listing for the Web source would look like this:

Campbell, Donna. "Frank Norris." *Naturalism in American Literature.* Washington State U, July 2005.

Web. 18 Aug. 2005.

An Authored Work in an Anthology

An anthology is a collection of works, often with multiple authors and editors. Always refer first to the specific author of the source within the anthology rather than to the editors or compilers. The exception is when you are referencing editorial commentary or notes. This first example refers to a short story by Michael Libling included in *The Year's Best Fantasy and Horror*:

The story "Puce Boy" employs the distinctive strategy of making colors tangible, interactive,

even deadly, as when Orry notes that, unlike primary pigments, "[i]n-between colors didn't kill"

(Libling 130).

This next reference (from the same text) comes from an introduction to a story by one of the editors:

Like Swift, who inspired the narrative approach we see in "Swiftly"—hence the pun in the title—

Roberts' material is both "droll" and "serious" in engaging ethical questions (Windling 283).

In this instance, the anthology cited has coeditors, Ellen Datlow and Terry Windling, but Windling is specifically indicated as the author of the quote above. On the works cited page, you would list Windling as the author of the quote but would still list both editors in the bibliographical entry, as follows:

Windling, Terry. Introduction to "Swiftly." *The Year's Best Fantasy and Horror.* 16th annual collec-

tion. Ed. Ellen Datlow and Terry Windling. New York: Griffin, 2003. 117. Print.

Indirect Sources

While it is always preferable to draw from and cite the original source, you may encounter situations in which the original is not readily available or is left uncertain in the source where you found it referenced. In this situation your own citation will use "qtd. in" (an abbreviated form of "quoted in") and then list the source from which the reference is drawn:

A primal tension between human culture and nature is present even among isolated African cul-

tures such as the Nandi. In one story, the embodiment of thunder admits to his primordial counter-

part, the elephant, "that he was afraid of man and said he would run away and go the heavens"

(qtd. in Sproul 48).

Multiple References Within a Citation

There may be occasions when you cite more than one source in a single sentence. For multiple sources, separate them within the parentheses by semicolons and follow standard rules otherwise:

...(Sproul 27; Erdoes 11; Abrahams 7).

For multiple references to a single source, use a comma to separate page numbers. The following paragraph uses three quotes from Clea Koff's *The Bone Woman* and cites them in sequence after the concluding quote mark:

> Koff explores some changes she underwent after investigating mass graves as a forensic anthropologist in Rwanda, Bosnia, Croatia, and Kosovo. "I was noticing that when I was talking about Kosovo I was talking about Rwanda, and when I was talking about the dead, I was also talking about the living, and when I was talking about me, I was also talking about the people in that room." She makes links across time, space, and cultures to dispel the notion that mass killing is "some tribal thing" and cannot happen here. Koff warns "it could happen anywhere, given the right ingredients" (259, 263, 264).

Authors with the Same Last Name

When citing authors with the same last name, you simply include the authors' first initials—or full first names in the situation where the authors share both last name and first initial(s)—along with the last name to distinguish between the authors. As always in MLA, give just enough information to clarify:

> ...(B. Alcott 57).

> ...(L. M. Alcott 113).

Literary Works of Various Editions

Well-established and widely known literary works are likely to have been reissued in numerous editions by various publishers. This means that the text will be available in a variety of formats and that pagination will vary widely. For this reason, it will be helpful to readers if you include more than a page-number reference in your citation. In the scholarly world, some specific edition of a literary work is nearly always preferred as the authoritative text. As a student research writer, you probably have more freedom to use any of a range of acceptable editions, but be aware that some teachers may expect the use of a designated scholarly edition. Find out whether there are such requirements before you begin your project.

For commonly taught and studied novels, include a chapter number after the page number and a semicolon:

> ...of *Far from the Madding Crowd* is a clear case in point (Hardy 99; ch. 19).

> **Note:** In the example above, the edition referred to renders chapter numbers in Roman numerals, but unlike the case of citing page numbers, MLA prefers conversion to Arabic numerals in such instances. The same is true for divisions within a play, as in our next example.

For plays, include (as relevant) the act, scene, and line numbers, each separated by periods. Arabic numerals are preferred here:

> All women in *Macbeth* are ultimately destroyed, leaving a barren land to the "bloody, bold, and resolute" men (4.1.95).

Note: Contemporary prose plays are unlikely to be published with the enumerated lines you see referenced in the example above. Simply use the page number in such cases.

For very long poems divided into enumerated sections (often books or cantos), include is designated divisions (where line numbering discontinues to begin anew in the next section) and line numbers, separated again by a period. The example below is for Ovid's *Metamorphoses*:

> ...(Ovid 6.680).

Or, alternatively, for shorter poems such as "Ulysses":

> ...(lines 33-43).

Once you have established that you are citing line numbers (and, in this case, those of Tennyson's "Ulysses") when referencing a particular poem, subsequent citations can omit the word "lines" and include just the number(s):

> ...(65-70).

Single-Page Sources and Works Compiled Alphabetically

A page number is not required when citing a one-page source. Cite the author within the text or in parentheses.

Some content of dictionaries and encyclopedias is regarded as "common knowledge" and may not need to be cited. When it is appropriate to cite from sources arranged alphabetically, such as dictionaries and encyclopedias, a page number is necessary only when the entry exceeds two pages in length, regardless of the number of pages in the volume containing the source referenced.

Interviews and Personal Communications

MLA requires no more than a source name for in-text citations for personal interviews and personal communications.

> ...(Fulton).

An e-mail, phone discussion, personal letter, or memorandum would be cited in the same way. See page 54 for the works cited format.

The Bible *and Other Sacred Texts*

Because of their special status and prominence, sacred texts represent a special case when it comes to citing them, and their titles are rarely indicated in the same way as titles of other published texts. Like some other titles, however, books of the Bible are abbreviated and then followed by specific references to chapter and verse (line), with periods separating them:

> . . . (*New Jerusalem Bible*, Rev. 11.3-13).

> **Note:** At the time this guide was written, the following Web page provided a list of standard abbreviations for various sections of the Bible: http://hbl.gcc.edu/abbreviationsMLA.htm

Once you have established that the translation or edition of the Bible you are citing (an accepted standard such as the King James, the New Jerusalem, or the New International Version), the title information can be excluded from subsequent citations:

> . . . (Gen. 1.23).

As shown above, the abbreviated book titles are not placed in quotation marks, and particular versions of the Bible are not italicized; the title of any published edition of the Bible, however, must be italicized when first cited in text as well as on your works cited page.

Tables and Illustrations

One last exception: for tables, graphs, illustrations, etc., the full bibliographic reference for the source should be provided directly underneath—even when it appears within the main text of your writing and is fully acknowledged on the works cited page.

Table 1

Proportion of Free Negroes, Whites, and Slaves Urban,* 1860

	Free Negroes	Whites	Slaves
United States	62.5%	51.2%	--
North	55.7%	48.5%	--
South	72.7%	68.7%	46.8%
Upper South	69.2%	69.4%	41.8%
Lower South	85.5%	66.7%	51.4%

* All places incorporated and unincorporated, greater than 2,500 in population.

Source: *Population of the United States in 1860*; Washington, DC, 1864.

Oral and Electronic Presentations

If you read a paper aloud or deliver an oral presentation that draws on outside sources, you should specifically cite the sources of information for direct and paraphrased material aloud as well. Most presenters dispense with page numbers when giving source information orally. One way to do this is to introduce the author's name and say aloud "quote" and "unquote" (or "end quote") to begin and end directly quoted material. Some people prefer to make the "air quote" sign (both hands up in a sort of modified peace sign, they waggle their fingers to begin and end the quotation). If the material is paraphrased, you can simply say something like: "according to . . ." or "as _____ claims." Some adept presenters can make clear the beginning and end of their source material just by vocal intonation, though it is probably best to err on the side of being explicit. Create a works cited page for a paper to be read aloud just as you would for a written essay.

When using print images (charts, pictures, maps, etc.), you should attach the source information to the image (or near it in cases where it might damage the document). It is also a good idea to identify the source aloud if it might be difficult for the audience to read from afar.

As with a paper that is read aloud, an electronic presentation should include a works cited page. The works cited page should be mentioned in the electronic presentation, but it is a good idea to bring at least one paper copy along. For electronic presentations, you may cite images and text parenthetically just as you would in a print essay. Software programs such as PowerPoint® give you a variety of ways to overlay text on, above, or below images. If your citation is clearly readable on or attached to the image, you do not need to read it aloud. For an example of how to cite an online image or movie, see the Web Publications section in Chapter 5.

Footnotes and Endnotes

MLA style permits the inclusion of either endnotes[1] or footnotes.[2] Notes provide additional explanatory information for your readers or elaborate on sources not directly pertinent to your own discussion. Both types of notes are provided as conveniences and courtesies for your readers: information vital to your own project should be directly cited and presented within the main text.

Notes

1. Endnotes are titled simply "Notes" and are compiled separately from the main essay and included just prior to your works cited page. Indent the first line five spaces and double-space the note.

---

2. Footnotes fall at the bottom of the page and provide information or references indirectly related to the focus of your own discussion and research. They are double-spaced and generally automatically formatted by your word processor.

4

Sample Student Paper with Works Cited Page

↕1 inch   ↓1/2 inch

Janie Evans

Professor Gonzales

Humanities 107

12 October 2008

Pocahontas: Less than Her Myth, More than a Myth

→ Many people have at least some familiarity with the mythical name

1/2 inch

Pocahontas before being introduced to the story of Jamestown when

they learn about U.S. history. Disney Studios' controversial adaptation of

the story of the young Indian "princess" and her fight to save the English

adventurer Captain John Smith, titled simply, *Pocahontas*, offers just

one of many popular culture depictions of this widely known but often

misunderstood Native American figure. We seem to want her part in our

American mythology to be that of the romantic heroine—beautiful, brave,

1 inch   1 inch

honorable, and devoted to her new love from across the seas. Such images

and expectations rely on severe distortions of situations and events, yet

Pocahontas did play an extremely significant role in colonial history.

She is an American hero because of the fact that she contributed to the

survival of the Jamestown settlers and was a crucial force in easing the

potentially explosive tensions between the English colonists in Virginia

and the confederation of native nations headed by her father, Powhatan.

Simultaneously, though, Pocahontas symbolizes the tragic consequences of

European colonization, whose impact obliterated traditional societies and

culture even when native peoples were able to survive and adapt.

Pocahontas was born in c.1596 as Matoaka to her clan and Amonte to

her parents; the nickname of Pocahontas has been translated as "playful one,"

but it has less positive associations in Algonquian usage, meaning "spoiled"

or "naughty child" (Crazy Horse). A favorite of her father, Chief Powhatan, she

↑1 inch

continued

(Proportions shown in this paper are adjusted to fit space limitations of this book. Follow actual dimensions discussed in this book and your instructor's directions.)

Evans 2

was by most accounts a vibrant personality who made a strong impression on all of the Jamestown colonists, including John Smith. Smith very nearly met with execution for insubordination on the trip over in 1607 at the hands of his own countrymen and was saved only by a set of sealed orders from the governing council in London naming him among the leaders of the new colony. This same arrogant, rowdy John Smith is the sole source for the first and most compelling episode in Pocahontas' myth.[1] The lone survivor of an ambushed hunting party, Smith reports that after several days in captivity he was brought before Powhatan, who ordered that he be put to death, but that fate, this time in the form of Pocahontas, once more came to his rescue:

1 inch

> [T]wo great stones were brought before Powhatan; then as many as could, laid hands on him, dragged him to them, and thereon laid his head and being ready with their clubs to beat out his brains, Pocahontas, the King's dearest daughter, when no entreaty could prevail, got his head in her arms and laid her own upon his to save him from death, whereat the Emperor [still referring to Powhatan] was contented....(Smith 48-51)

Pocahontas believed that the Indians had things to learn from the English (*Pocahontas, Her True Story*).

Historians question whether or not Smith's life was actually in danger, as he reports it, or whether he misconstrued a ritualistic pageant (Allen), yet Pocahontas may have intervened at another point by necessity: there is some evidence that she acted as "an informer for

---

1. Smith never mentions Pocahontas in any of his writings prior to her death in 1617. This fact has been mentioned frequently in any number of analyses of the events reported. The general trend of many of these is to suggest that Smith invented, or at least embroidered, the story, as part of a campaign of promotional propaganda to encourage colonization.

the colony, warning Smith of her father's belligerent plans" when Powhatan threatened Smith's life in 1608 (Henrico County). At the very least it seems clear that Pocahontas established an early pattern of intervening on behalf of Smith and the English colonists.

Like so many other early colonies, Jamestown was beset with troubles of every kind, and like every other previous English colony, it came very near to complete collapse. Pocahontas was prominent among those who directly helped the colonists avoid starvation. Tradition holds that she and Smith remained on friendly terms—though nothing indicates intimate relations between them at any point—but there are no other recorded details of direct interactions between Pocahontas and Smith prior to her own visit to England in 1616; Smith himself returned in 1609.[2] Knowledge of Pocahontas' activities becomes historically vague between then and 1613, when she was kidnapped by the Jamestown colonists (having been lured aboard a ship in the Potomac by two of her own people in exchange for manufactured goods, if accounts are valid) and used as a political tool against Powhatan. She does not appear to have been directly abused or mistreated, but she was held for an extended length of time. During this captivity, Pocahontas converted to Christianity, a fact that contrasts sharply with the ideal depicted by Disney in 1995, which glorifies the supposed persistence of native spirituality: "O Great Spirit, hear our song / Help us keep the ancient ways / Keep the sacred fire strong / Walk in balance all our days" (Schwartz lines 13-16). She is believed to be the first Native American to so convert, and she was baptized with the given name of Rebecca in 1613.

---

2. They did, however, meet again in London, when she visited with husband John Rolfe in 1616. Smith claims that the meeting was cordial. Other evidence indicates some ill will toward Smith on Pocahontas' part (Crazy Horse).

continued

Around this time, one of the colonists, widower John Rolfe, took a "special interest" in Pocahontas, and they were married in 1614 with the apparent blessings of Powhatan and the governor of Virginia (qtd. in Crazy Horse). Some historians remain suspicious of Rolfe's motives since tobacco profits were involved, but a relative peace did follow between Powhatan's people and the colonists for the next several years. Rolfe and Rebecca/Pocahontas had a son, Thomas, in 1615, and in 1616 the Virginia Company encouraged the family to visit England. Upon their arrival, Pocahontas was presented to King James I and Queen Anne, along with many other high-society members among whom she was deemed a princess.[3] She is rumored to have captivated poet and playwright Ben Jonson (Ross 35-36), and it was during this stay that the famous Simon van de Passe engraving was done—the only such portrait in existence (Virginia Historical Society). All of this served to enhance and strengthen the emerging myth.

Then in 1617, at the young age of twenty-two, just when her family was to return to Virginia, Pocahontas became very ill and died suddenly. It is actually uncertain how she died; some historians suggest smallpox, others say tuberculosis or pneumonia. She was buried in Gravesend, England. John Rolfe would return to Virginia alone, leaving Thomas to be raised and educated by his family in England. Powhatan himself died the next spring. Without Pocahontas' presence and efforts, the always uneasy relations in Virginia eroded over the next several years, and eventually degenerated into destructive warfare.

The story of Pocahontas has been called a myth, and most of us expect the key figure in a myth to be a hero, who, as Mossiker states, has

---

3. Chief Roy Crazy Horse reminds his readers that royalty in the European sense never existed among Powhatan nations and that this was a further romantic contrivance.

"relevance to ... [a people's] origins, survival, development, happiness or glory" (11). By this definition, she can be called an American hero because she helped keep the Virginia colony afloat, establishing the first successful English outpost in America. As a result, more colonists were inspired to take the adventure across the Atlantic to a "New World." Speaking on behalf of the contemporary Powhatan Nation, however, Chief Roy Crazy Horse states that the mythical figure popularized by Disney is "the hero of Euro-Americans ... [,] the 'good Indian'" used to help justify historical abuses against Native American rights.

Pocahontas herself has no say in the myth. Historians and special interests have pieced together her tale from scant documentation and Smith's questionable *General History* in support of their own agendas. The subsequent pictorial history—marked by a progressive softening, whitening, and, finally, abandoning of the native features captured by Van de Passe—perhaps most clearly demonstrates this (Ross). Regardless of how Pocahontas' contributions are perceived, for a woman—particularly such a youthful Native American woman—to have had such an impact on our history is amazing in an otherwise male-dominated arena. Pocahontas at the age of twelve was giving advice to her father, acting as a liaison between dramatically different cultures, and perhaps even serving as a spy for either or both sides. She is both more and less than the popular myth. She will remain simultaneously an icon of America's success and a tragic reminder of the cost at which it came.

Works Cited

Allen, Paula Gunn. *Pocahontas*: *Medicine Woman, Spy, Entrepreneur, Diplomat*. San Francisco: Harper, 2003. Print.

Crazy Horse, Chief Roy. "The Pocahontas Myth." *Campfire Stories*. Manataka American Indian Council, May 2003. Web. 24 Sept. 2008.

Henrico County. "The Four Faces of Pocahontas." Board of Supervisors and County Manager's Office, Henrico County, VA, n.d. Web. 24 Sept. 2008.

Mossiker, Frances. *Pocahontas*. New York: Knopf, 1976. Print.

Pocahontas. Dir. Mike Gabriel and Eric Goldberg. Walt Disney Studios, 1995. DVD.

Pocahontas, Her True Story. Screenplay and dir. Jonathan Gili. BBC: Worldwide Americans, 1995. Videocassette.

Ross, John F. "Picturing Pocahontas." *Smithsonian* Jan. 1999: 34-36. Print.

Schwartz, Stephen, and Alan Menken. "Steady as the Beating Drum." *Pocahontas*. Dir. Mike Gabriel and Eric Goldberg. Walt Disney Studios, 1995. DVD.

Smith, John. *General History of Virginia, New England, and the Summer Isles*. *The Norton Anthology of American Literature*. Ed. Nina Baym et al. Shorter 6th ed. New York: Norton, 2003. 44-53. Print.

Virginia Historical Society. "Contact and Conflict." *The Story of Virginia, an American Experience*. Virginia Historical Society, Online Exhibitions, n.d. Web. 29 Sept. 2008.

Creating a Works Cited Page

Key Terms

Author   The writer, creator, or originator of a source. There may be a single author, multiple authors, or a corporate entity listed as the author. The author is the identifier for a source, both in-text and in the works cited section—indeed, the word "authority" is derived from "author." Works with no listed author, particularly **secondary sources**, should be used sparingly and with skepticism.

Bibliography   A list of key sources relating to a particular subject or area of research. It differs from a list of works cited in that it goes beyond the sources specifically cited within a particular piece of scholarship to provide a broad list of the sources used or consulted during the research process. Most bibliographies are labeled "Selected Bibliography" because few can claim to be a complete list of pertinent sources. An "Annotated Bibliography" provides a brief description (or abstract) of each listed source.

Edition   The particular version of a source; multiple editions indicate either periodic updates, as with many standardized textbooks, or a varied publication history, as is often the case with "public domain" (originally published prior to the emergence of modern copyright laws) literary texts. If no edition or editorial information appears on a title page, you can assume that the source is a first edition or a reprint thereof. However, if you were to cite Charles Brockden Brown's 1798 novel *Wieland* in an essay, you'd find that a modern edition likely has an editor, an introduction, and possibly an afterword. (Such editorial supplements are cited differently from how the text itself is cited: see our examples for in-text and works cited listings.) A text that has been updated, revised, or abridged will be given a different edition designation, for example, 3rd ed., Rev. ed., or Abr. ed.

Medium   The format or the means of conveying information. For published print information, "Print" is the medium; for electronic sources, "Web," "CD-ROM," or "Diskette"; for broadcasts, "Radio" or "Television"; for sound recordings, "Audiocassette," "LP," or "CD"; for film or video, "Film," "Videocassette," or "DVD"; and for a live play, opera, or concert, "Performance." For visual art sources, describe the material of composition, such as "Photograph," "Marble," "Graphite on paper," "Ceramic," "Oil on canvas," etc.

Periodical   Newspapers, magazines, and journals are called "periodicals" because they are published at regular intervals (daily, weekly, monthly, quarterly, etc.). Other works not published at regular intervals—books, pamphlets, and many Web sources such as home pages, digitized print material, and on-line postings—may be referred to as "nonperiodical" publications.

Primary and Secondary Source   A **primary source** is a direct item of evidence pertaining to the subject under discussion, or, in the case of literary or artistic criticism, it is the actual text being critiqued. Other examples of primary sources include information from an experiment you conducted, data from a survey you administered, or (in most cases) a historical document you retrieved from an archive. A **secondary source** presents external, after-the-fact commentary, research, or analysis relevant to your research topic. Secondary sources provide access to the expertise of professionals in any given field and allow you to benefit from previous research in the area. For example, in an essay about class distinctions in *Twelfth Night*, Shakespeare's play would be a primary source, as would commentary on class issues by one of his contemporaries or a woodcut bearing a scene illustrating the concept. By contrast, a modern article by Anne Barton on the subject would be a secondary source. When you write a research paper for a college course, you add a secondary source to the world of information.

Publisher   The agency, entity, or individual sponsoring the production and circulation of (usually) written materials. Such alternative media as film and music have terminology and distribution channels distinct to those industries, but the parallel remains valid. Publication presses might reside within a reputable university that lends their publications credibility, or they might operate in the private sector as trade publishers, where profit is the driving force and *caveat emptor* ("let the buyer beware") is the rule. In the case of newspapers and other periodicals, the name of the publisher is that of the publication itself, such as the *New York Times*, so no additional publisher need be indicated in your works cited list. Be leery of self-published materials or Web-based publications lacking affiliation or substantiation (see the Evaluating Print Sources section in Chapter 2).

Scholarly Journal (and Peer Review)   Scholarly journals are carefully edited for verifiable content, proper attribution and use of sources, and significance within the fields they cover. They are generally published quarterly (or even less frequently) and contain articles by professionals and experts. They are generally also peer reviewed, which means that other experts read and comment on submissions before they are accepted for publication or rejected. Their high level of professionalism, article selection, and editing make scholarly journals excellent secondary sources. They often include both **volume** and **issue** numbers.

Volume and Issue Scholarly journals typically consider one year's cycle of publication as a "volume," and each "issue" of the journal that comes out during the year as part of that volume. For this reason, scholarly journals frequently use continuous pagination—for example, if issue 1 of a certain year ends on page 136, then issue 2 will begin on page 137. Cite both volume and issue numbers whenever they are available.

Web Publication Anything published on the World Wide Web. Because this includes a very diverse range of material, MLA uses the following categories to help identify and cite sources:

> **Nonperiodical Online Publications**. Online sources not published on a set time schedule. Home pages, weblog (blog) postings, digitized books and movies, course materials, dissertations and theses, and reviews are all examples.
> **Periodical Online Publications**. A journal or "zine" that is periodically published only on the Web and which has no print counterpart.
> **Periodical Print Publications in an Online Database**. Print newspapers, magazines, and journals available online through databases such as ProQuest, Academic Search Premier, and JSTOR, to name only a few. Check out your library's access to databases—full-text availability of sources is a relatively new, very convenient function of some databases.

The Works Cited Section

As we have indicated previously, research essays done in the MLA style must conclude with a works cited section that lists every source to which you have referred in the body of your paper (an example appears on page 40). As the term *works cited* indicates, only the works directly cited during your discussion are listed here, and each in-text citation incorporated into your essay must correspond to an entry listed among your works cited.

Let us emphasize this: EVERY SOURCE LISTED IN YOUR WORKS CITED PAGE MUST BE REFERENCED WITHIN THE BODY OF YOUR ESSAY. This distinguishes a **works cited** section from a **bibliography**—a listing of all sources consulted or reviewed during the research process such as you may have been required to compile at other points in your educational career.

Works cited entries are alphabetized so that your reader can immediately match a source reference within your essay to the complete bibliographic information for that source. Alphabetize sources by the last name of each author (start with the first author listed when there are more than one); by the first substantive word (ignore the articles "The," "An," and "A") in a corporate author's name; or by the first substantive word of the source's title when no author's name is given. Citations made within the text of your essay should match up with these entries because you have used the same author or title names in every instance.

Your works cited section should be formatted as follows (see the example on page 40):

- It should stand alone as the last section of your research paper, separate from the main text, tables, graphs, illustrations, and any endnotes. It should be titled "Works Cited," centered at the top of the page, and the first entry should begin one double-spaced increment below the title.
- It should be alphabetized according to each author's last name or the first substantive word of the title when no author is listed (ignore "A," "An," and "The").
- Each alphabetized entry should begin with the first line flush with the left margin and subsequent lines indented five spaces. This reversal of standard indentation allows names to stand out for easy location.
- The entire section should be double-spaced with no additional space between entries.

A typical entry for a **print source** will require the following:

Author's Last Name, First Name. *Full Italicized Title of the Work*. City or Other Place of Publication: Name of Publisher, Year of Publication. Medium of Publication "Print".

There are various exceptions and additions to this basic format, which the following examples are designed to cover; they include the majority of print sources you will most frequently use and cite in your research writing.

Printed Books

Books with a single author generally follow the formula given above. Your information should be drawn from the **title page**, not from the cover of the book.

Book with One Author

Morrow, James. *The Philosopher's Apprentice*. New York: Harper, 2008. Print.

Book with Two or Three Authors

Levitt, Steven D., and Stephen J. Dubner. *Freakonomics: A Rogue Economist Explores the Hidden Side of Everything*. New York: Morrow-Harper, 2005. Print.

Book with Four or More Authors

For the sake of brevity and convenience, MLA style allows for the abbreviation of a group of more than three authors. Following the full name of the first listed author, "et al." (meaning "and others") is used.

> Bellah, Robert N., et al. *Habits of the Heart: Individualism and Commitment*
>> *in American Life*. New York: Harper, 1985. Print.

Be aware of the distinction between authors, translators, and editors, especially when dealing with anthologies.

A Translated Book

> St. Mery, Moreau de. *Moreau de St. Mery's American Journey*. Trans. Kenneth Roberts and Anna M.
>> Roberts. New York: Doubleday, 1947. Print.

An Edited Book—Introduction, Foreword, Preface, or Afterword

Your works cited listing for an edited collection or text will depend on how you are using the work. If you refer to a work within an edited collection that was not authored by the collection's editor, alphabetize your entry according to the author's name:

> Fiedler, Jean, and Jim Melee. "Asimov's Robots." *Critical Encounters: Writers and Themes in*
>> *Science Fiction*. Ed. Dick Riley. New York: Ungar, 1978. 1-22. Print.

Since this entry assumes that an essay within the collection is being cited, the editor is not named until after the title information. "Ed." in this example denotes "edited by," which differs from "ed." meaning "edition." Notice that both the title of the essay and that of the larger collection must be listed. Notice also that because a shorter complete work within a larger collection is being referenced, page numbers must be included. If, however, you were to cite an editor's commentary in an introduction, foreword, or afterword, you would do it this way:

> Riley, Dick. Foreword. *Critical Encounters: Writers and Themes in Science Fiction*. Ed. Riley. New
>> York: Ungar, 1978. vii-viii. Print.

A Collection of Works by One Author

Individual works drawn from one text must be listed separately with the full-text title. Notice, that the author's name is listed only with the first alphabetized source. All additional listings for that author replace the name with three hyphens and a period, as in the second example on page 47:

> O'Hara, Frank. "Alma." *The Selected Poems of Frank O'Hara*. Ed. Donald Allen.
>> New York: Vintage, 1974. 47-49. Print.

2 Title

3 Subtitle

1 Authors

5 Publisher

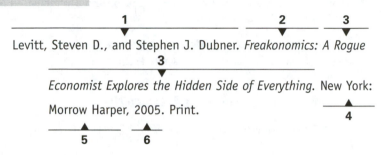

6 Date of Publication

> FREAKONOMICS. Copyright © 2005 by Steven D. Levitt and Stephen J. Dubner.
> All rights reserved. Printed in the United States of America. No part of this book may be used
> or reproduced in any manner whatsoever without written permission except in the case of brief
> quotations embodied in critical articles and reviews. For information address HarperCollins
> Publishers Inc., 10 East 53rd Street, New York, NY 10022.
>
> HarperCollins books may be purchased for educational, business, or sales promotional use.
> For information please write: Special Markets Department, HarperCollins Publishers Inc.,
> 10 East 53rd Street, New York, NY 10022.
>
> FIRST EDITION

4 Place of Publication

1

Levitt, Steven D., and Stephen J. Dubner. *Freakonomics: A Rogue*
3
Economist Explores the Hidden Side of Everything. New York:
Morrow Harper, 2005. Print.
5   6

> **Note:** The first (alphabetized) author's name is the only name in an entry that is listed
> "last name first." This standard applies to all non-alphabetized names within an entry.
> Note here, too, that "New York" refers to the city, not the state.

---. "Blocks." *The Selected Poems of Frank O'Hara.* Ed. Donald Allen. New York:
Vintage, 1974. 46-47. Print.

Two (or More) Books by the Same Author

It is commonplace for well-established and widely known literary works, to
go through a number of different editions. MLA requires you to list both the
original publication date (immediately after the title) and the date for the
edition you used (at the end).

Pynchon, Thomas. *The Crying of Lot 49.* 1965. New York: Harper, 1990. Print.

---. *Gravity's Rainbow.* 1973. New York: Bantam, 1976. Print.

A Republished Book with an Editor

James, Henry. *The Wings of the Dove.* 1902. Ed. J. Donald Crowley and Richard A. Hocks. New
York: Norton, 1978. Print.

Book with a Title Within a Title

To denote another book's title within a title, simply remove the italics from it:

Macpherson, Pat. *Reflecting on* The Bell Jar. New York: Routledge, 1991. Print.

An alternative way to denote another book's title within a title is to identify it with quotation marks:

Macpherson, Pat. *Reflecting on "The Bell Jar."* New York: Routledge, 1991. Print.

If the title within a title is of a shorter work (set in quotation marks), simply keep the quotation marks.

Connolly, Thomas E. *Nathaniel Hawthorne: "Young Goodman Brown."* Columbus: Merrill, 1968. Print.

Book with a Corporate Author

A corporate group or entity is treated as a single author and alphabetized by the first substantive word in its name or title.

American Heart Association. *Living Well, Staying Well: The Ultimate Guide to Help Prevent Heart Disease and Cancer.* New York: Potter, 1998. Print.

Book Authored under a Pseudonym (an Assumed Name)

Brent, Linda [Harriot Brent Jacobs]. *Incidents in the Life of a Slave Girl.* 1861. Orlando: Harcourt, 1973. Print.

Graphic Novels

Graphic narratives are sometimes the work of several people and sometimes the product of a single author-illustrator. Treat a single author-illustrator like you would treat an author in any other print novel entry (see the Smith entry below), but list the roles of contributors in a collaborative work. Begin your entry with the person's name and role most pertinent to your research, (say, art and artist), as in the Gibbons example below.

Gibbons, Dave, illus. *Watchmen.* By Alan Moore. Ed. Barry Marx. New York: DC Comics, 1995. Print.

Smith, Jeff. *Bone: The Complete Cartoon in One Edition.* Columbus: Cartoon Books, 2004. Print.

Book with an Unknown Author

The Mabinogion. Trans. Jeffrey Gantz. New York: Penguin, 1976. Print.

An Anthology in Subsequent Editions

Students who look at the cover of the book they are citing and list the name they see there as the author of their source make one of the most common errors in citation. When citing an anthology, be sure to cite the author of the individual work you are using, not the editor:

> Alexie, Sherman. "Flight Patterns." *The Norton Introduction to Literature*. Ed.
> Alison Booth et al. 9th ed. New York: Norton, 2005. 133-41. Print.

Book in a Series

Note that the title of the series comes after the medium of publication, "Print" in this example, a rare exception to the general rule.

> Arvin, Newton. *Herman Melville*. New York: Sloane, 1950. Print. The American
> Men of Letters Ser. 3.

Multivolume Works

> Behn, Aphra. *The Works of Aphra Behn*. Ed. Montague Summers. 1915. Vol. 3.
> New York: Blom, 1967. Print.

Sacred Texts

> *The New Oxford Annotated Bible: New Revised Standard Version*. Ed. Michael D.
> Coogan et al. 3rd ed. New York: Oxford UP, 2001. Print.

> *Tanakh, a New Translation of the Holy Scriptures According to the Traditional*
> *Hebrew Text*. Philadelphia: Jewish Publication Society, 1985. Print.

Dictionaries

As a general rule, the best advice for quoting dictionaries is *don't*. Unless the word is obscure or has changed in meaning over time (e.g., "pretend" can mean "to aspire to"), it is considered **common knowledge** (see the Key Terms in Chapter 3) and you do not need to cite it. Resist the urge to begin an essay by citing a dictionary unless the word is truly one your instructor is unlikely to know—this may include arcane medical terminology, recent slang, specific legal terms, etc. *The Oxford English Dictionary*, widely considered the most authoritative dictionary, covers word origins and usage over time (etymology). Use your desk dictionary often, but cite it sparingly.

> "Fardel." *The Oxford English Dictionary*. 2nd ed. 1989. Print.

When using a less common or more specialized dictionary, give a full citation:

> "Installation Art." *The Yale Dictionary of Art and Artists*. Ed. Erika Langmuir
> and Norbert Lynton. New Haven: Yale UP, 2000. Print.

Encyclopedias

Like dictionaries, encyclopedia entries are generally arranged alphabetically, so there is no need to cite page numbers. If the entry has a named author, list the author's name first as you would with any other source. If you are using a common reference book—such as *The Encyclopaedia Britannica* or *The Encyclopedia Americana*—you need list only the term, title, and year of the edition:

"Seneca Falls Convention." *The Encyclopedia Americana*. 1994 ed. Print.

As with dictionary citations, give full information for more specialized reference sources.

"Frost, Robert." *Benet's Reader's Encyclopedia of American Literature.* Ed. George Perkins, Barbara Perkins, and Phillip Leininger. New York: Harper, 1991. Print.

Print Periodicals

Periodicals are publications that appear on a regular schedule (daily, weekly, monthly, quarterly). Newspapers, magazines, and journals (scholarly, trade, opinion) are all periodicals. Periodicals require more specific date of publication information than books, including the day in the case of most newspapers.

Newspaper Articles

Some newspapers, such as *USA Today* and the *New York Times*, come out in different editions in different parts of the country. These editions are usually indicated at the top of page 1, on the masthead: "natl. ed.," "late ed.," "western ed.," "overseas ed.," etc. This supplemental edition information is listed between the date and the page numbers in your citation. Use abbreviations for all months except May, June, and July. If the article is not on sequential pages—for example, if it starts on page A1 and continues on A9—place a + after the page where it begins: A1+. Drop the first article in a newspaper's name: for example, *The New York Times* will become *New York Times* in your works cited list.

Semple, Kirk. "Iraqis Stunned by the Violence of a Bombing." *New York Times* 18 July 2005, natl. ed.: A1+. Print.

Print Source from a Web Archive

The same source, obtained from a Web archive, would be cited in this way:

Semple, Kirk. "Iraqis Stunned by the Violence of a Bombing." *New York Times* 18 July 2005, late ed.: A1+. *ProQuest*. Web. 28 July 2008.

Editorials

"Shame on Iran." Editorial. *New York Times* 28 Aug. 2009, late ed.: A22. Print.

Reviews

Donahue, Deirdre. Rev. of *The Lady and the Panda,* by Vicki Constantine Croke. *USA Today* 2 Aug. 2005: D5. Print.

Popular Magazines and Journals

The format here is similar to that used with newspapers: **Author. "Title."** *Publication* **Date: page numbers. Medium.** If the magazine does not list an author for the particular article of interest to you, begin with the title. Do not list volume or issue numbers (except for scholarly journals—see below). As with newspaper citations, drop the first article: *The Economist* becomes *Economist*. Give additional information directly after the article title, such as whether it is an interview, a review ("Rev. of..."), or a letter to the editor. Note that, unlike book titles, no period follows a periodical title. As with a newspaper entry, if the article does not appear on sequential pages, give the first page number and a plus sign (example: 59+).

Weekly Publications

"Anniversary Lessons from eBay." *Economist* 11 June 2005: 9. Print.

Book Review in a Weekly Publication

Grossman, Lev. Rev. of *The Ruins*, by Scott Smith. *Time* 24 July 2006: 59. Print.

Movie Review in a Weekly Publication

Lane, Anthony. "Beautiful Friendships." Rev. of *The Edge of Heaven,* dir. Fatih
    Akin. *New Yorker* 26 May 2008: 88-89. Print.

Monthly Magazines

Connors, Jill. "A Light Touch." *This Old House* Sept. 2004: 112-19. Print.

Magazines Covering Two or More Months

Lobell, Jarrett. "Naples Underground." *Archeology* May-June 2008: 22-28. Print.

Quarterly Publications

Namkung, Bonnie. "Bodies in Motion." *Artisan Northwest* Summer 2005: 17-19. Print.

Scholarly Journals

Scholarly journals are aimed at professionals and students in a specific field and tend to be more serious in tone and subject matter than popular magazines. They are generally edited and refereed by people who have risen to the top of their professions (a process called "peer review") and are considered strong research sources. One difference between citing a scholarly journal and a magazine is that you will cite both the volume and the issue numbers of journals. Some separately paginated journals will have only a volume number while others will have only an issue number—cite volume and issue numbers, as provided, before the date. See page 53.

> Brockmeier, Jens. "Texts and Other Symbolic Spaces." *Mind, Culture, and*
> > *Activity* 8.3 (2001): 215-30. Print.

Continuous Pagination

Many journals start with page 1 at the beginning of their publishing year and continuously number the pages of each issue until the final page of the last issue of the year. For this reason you may find an issue that begins with page 345 and ends on page 460.

> Malphurs, Ryan. "The Media's Frontier Construction of President George W.
> > Bush." *Journal of American Culture* 31.2 (2008): 185-201. Print.

Separate Pagination

When each new issue begins with page 1, listing the issue number is essential. Note the title within a title in the example below.

> Fullard, Katja. "Gender Images in Dieter Wellerschoff's Der Liebeswunch." *Rocky*
> > *Mountain Review of Language and Literature* 59.1 (2005): 47-62. Print.

Other Print Sources

Pamphlets and Brochures

> *Tolerance and Identity: Jews in Early New York, 1654-1825.* New York: Museum
> > of the City of New York, 2005. Print.

Government Publications

When citing government publications, treat the specific government (federal, state, county, city) and agency as the author. Government publications often require more patience and fortitude to research because of their great quantity and density. Many federal government publications come from the Government Printing Office (GPO) in Washington DC, which publishes bills, resolutions, reports, and miscellaneous documents from the House and Senate. Here are some common abbreviations you may run into when researching government documents: Congressional Record—Cong. Rec.; House of Representatives—H or HR; Senate—S or Sen.; resolution—Res.; document—Doc.; and department—Dept.

> United States. Dept. of Health and Human Services. *The Surgeon General's Report on Nutrition*
> > *and Health.* Washington: GPO, 1988. Print.

> Washington Dept. of Fish and Wildlife. "Marine Area Rules." *Sport Fishing Rules 2005/2006.*
> > Pamphlet ed. 2005. Print.

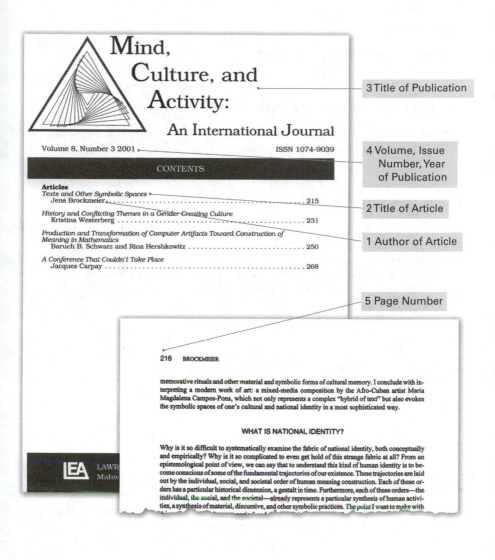

Mind, Culture, and Activity:

An International Journal

Volume 8, Number 3 2001   ISSN 1074-9039

3 Title of Publication

4 Volume, Issue Number, Year of Publication

CONTENTS

2 Title of Article

1 Author of Article

5 Page Number

216   BROCKMEIER

memorative rituals and other material and symbolic forms of cultural memory. I conclude with interpreting a modern work of art: a mixed-media composition by the Afro-Cuban artist Maria Magdalena Campos-Pons, which not only represents a complex "hybrid of text" but also evokes the symbolic spaces of one's cultural and national identity in a most sophisticated way.

WHAT IS NATIONAL IDENTITY?

Why is it so difficult to systematically examine the fabric of national identity, both conceptually and empirically? Why is it so complicated to even get hold of this strange fabric at all? From an epistemological point of view, we can say that to understand this kind of human identity is to become conscious of some of the fundamental trajectories of our existence. These trajectories are laid out by the individual, social, and societal order of human meaning construction. Each of these orders has a particular historical dimension, a gestalt in time. Furthermore, each of these orders—the individual, the social, and the societal—already represents a particular synthesis of human activities, a synthesis of material, discursive, and other symbolic practices. The point I want to make with

LEA   LAWR
    Mahw

Brockmeier, J. (2001). Texts and other symbolic spaces. *Mind, Culture, and Activity; An International Journal,* 8, 215-230.

Dissertations

Pringle, Michael W. "Seizing the Moral High Ground: The Discourses of Alcohol
in American Literature." Diss. Washington State U, 2000. Print.

Published Proceedings of a Conference

Tammany, Jane E. "Peer Gynt: 'In the Desert.'" *Proceedings of the International Conference in
Comparative Drama, 22 Oct. 1982, American U.* Ed. David Konstan and Charlotte
Shabrawy. Cairo: American U in Cairo, 1984. Print.

Legal Documents

Legal citations are full of obscure abbreviations and can be difficult to cite fully
and correctly. Citing such sources is beyond the scope of this book except in their
most basic forms. *The Bluebook: A Uniform System of Citation* is the definitive
source for the citation of legal documents. You can refer to famous court cases
such as *Roe v. Wade* and *Brown v. Board of Education* simply by name. Here are
two basic citations:

Constitution

US Const. Art. 3, sec. 3. Print.

Supreme Court Rulings

Zacchini v. Scripps-Howard Broadcasting Co. 433 US 562, 97. Supreme Court of the US. 1977.
Print.

Personal Communications

An unpublished letter is labeled "manuscript" ("MS") for the medium. An e-mail
version is handled slightly differently, as shown below.

Hammond, Alex. Letter to the author. 15 Nov. 2006. MS.

Hammond, Alex. Message to Michael Pringle. 12 Dec. 2007. E-mail.

Published Letters

Adams, Abigail. "To John Adams." 19 Aug. 1774. *Adams Family Correspondence.* Ed. L. H.
Butterfield et al. Vol. 6. Cambridge: Harvard UP, 1963-93.   Print.

Cartoons

Wilson, Gahan. Cartoon. *New Yorker* 27 June 2005: 65. Print.

Maps and Charts

Embryonic Stem Cell Lines. Chart. *National Geographic* July 2005: 23. Print.

Heart of the Middle East. Map. Washington: National Geographic Society, 2002. Print.

Manuscripts and Typescripts

When citing an original handwritten manuscript (MS) or typescript (TS), you must list the form, the title of the collection (if it has one), and where the collection is located (city).

Hopkins, Gerard Manley. "Inversnaid." N.d. MS. Gerard Manley Hopkins
Collection. Gonzaga, Spokane.

Note: In the example above, as with the interview citation below, the medium label does not end the citation.

Non-Print Sources

Personal Interview

When you interview someone in person, specify "Personal interview." Use "Telephone interview" or "E-mail interview" when appropriate.

Walter, Jess. Personal interview. 12 Aug. 2007.

Radio or Television Interview

Greenburg, Jan Crawford. Interview by Gwen Ifill. *The News Hour with Jim
Lehrer.* PBS. KSPS, Spokane. 27 June 2005. Television.

Film

When citing a film, name those whose contributions you are discussing and specify their titles or roles in the film. For example, Orson Welles is both the director and the main actor in his version of *Macbeth*. List the screenwriter first if his or her work is your focus—the same is true for costuming, set design, photography, special effects, etc. If you are discussing the film in more general terms, begin with the film's title, and then list both the director and the principal actors. "Dir." is short for "directed by" and "Perf." is an abbreviation of "performed by." List the medium as "Film."

Charlie and the Chocolate Factory. Dir. Tim Burton. Perf. Johnny Depp, Freddy Highmore, Helena
Bonham Carter, and Christopher Lee. Warner Bros., 2005. Film.

Videotape or DVD

The Merchant of Venice. Dir. Michael Radford. Perf. Al Pacino, Jeremy Irons,
Joseph Fiennes, and Lynn Collins. 2004. Sony Pictures, 2005. DVD.

Welles, Orson, dir. *Macbeth*. Perf. Orson Welles, Roddy McDowell, and Jeannette Nolan. 1948. Republic Pictures, 1992. Videocassette.

Live Performance

Fences. By August Wilson. Dir. Leah Gardiner. Perf. Charles Robinson, Shona Tucker, Josiah Phillips, and Kevin Kenerly. Angus Bowmer Theater, Ashland. 8 May 2008. Performance.

Lecture, Speech, Reading, or Address

In addition to name and title, give location, date, and descriptive title such as "Address," "Keynote speech," "Lecture," or "Reading."

Chomsky, Noam. "America's Quest for Global Dominance." Martin Center, Spokane. 21 Apr. 2005. Lecture.

Sound Recording

List: **Artist(s).** *Title*. **Manufacturer. Date. Medium.** For medium, use "Audiocassette," "Audiotape," "CD," or "LP." "CD" stands for "compact disc" and "LP" for "long-playing record." Where appropriate you may also use "Comp." for "composed by" and "Cond." for "conducted by." If you download music from the Web, list "Web" as the medium and give the date of access: Web. 20 Sept. 2008.

The Police. *Synchronicity*. A&M Records, 1983. Audiocassette.

Wonder, Stevie. *Natural Wonder*. Motown, 1995. CD.

Artwork

If you visit the actual artwork, list the artist's name, title of work, date of composition (use "N.d." if unknown), medium of composition, institution displaying the work, and location. When using an image from a published text, omit the original medium of composition and include the title and publishing information for the source.

Bernini, Gianlorenzo. *Rape of Proserpine*. N.d. Marble. Museo e Galleria Borghese, Rome.

Rubens, Peter-Paul. *Life of Marie de Médicis*. 1622. Louvre, Paris. *Paris: City of Art*. Ed. Jean Marie Pérouse de Montclos. New York: Vendome, 2000. 254. Print.

Web and Electronic Publications

It has been said that you can never step into the same river twice, and the same is true for the Internet. It is a constantly changing venue, where information is transitory and can disappear without notice. Even when information endures, it may appear on different sites in different stages of update and with different links. There are thus fewer standards for citing publication information from Web sites than there are for print sources, and this can lead to problems in clearly identifying sources. Furthermore, electronic forms are always evolving, making a standard method for citing them difficult to establish. In many ways the Web represents the Wild West of research sources; nonetheless, the basic citation formula remains similar to that used for print sources.

The Modern Language Association once required the inclusion of the full **URL** (Uniform Resource Locator) for each Web source citation. Because URLs are cumbersome and often of limited value, MLA now recommends including a URL only when the source might be difficult to find without it. For example, the Hall source cited below is one of many pages listed under the name "Chris Hall." A problem with some word processing programs (when you are trying to make a list of works cited) is that they automatically format a URL as a link. If your program does this, either turn off the automatic function or "undo" the automatic format each time you type a URL. URL information can be excessively long, too, so it is better to give the address of the database's home page or search page rather than list a URL with one hundred or more characters. **Include a URL only if it will be difficult for a reader to find the source without it.** (Chapter 2 explains how to read and evaluate a URL.)

> Hall, Chris. *Chris Hall's Home Page*. 26 Oct. 2002. Web. 10 Feb. 2004. <http://www.geocities.
> com/scrummy757>.

The following examples are offered as a guide to citing Web publications. But be aware that citation standards will continue to change as technology changes, and one way to track citation style changes is to visit the Modern Language Association's Web site <www.mla.org>.

> Modern Language Association. "How Do I Document Sources from the Web in the Works-Cited
> List for My Research Paper?" *Modern Language Association*. MLA, 29 Apr. 2008. Web. 1
> Aug. 2008.

Web-Exclusive Sources

For a Web-exclusive source, one with no print counterpart, use the following criteria to create a proper citation. While much of the information is parallel to the information given for print sources, there are some differences, and a couple of new abbreviations. For example, "n.p." is used if no publisher or sponsor is listed for the site, "n. pag." is used when there are no page numbers, and "n.d." is used when there is no listed date of publication.

> Name of Author, Editor, Compiler, etc. "Title of Document." *Overall Web Site Title*. Edition or
> version. Publisher or Sponsor, Date of Publication. Medium ["Web"]. Date of Access.

> American Heart Association. "Healthy Lifestyle." *American Heart Association, Learn and Live*.
> AHA, 2008. Web. 10 July 2008.

> Tietje, Louise. "Hegemonic Visualism." *Radical Pedagogy* June 2005: n. pag. Web. 5 Aug. 2008.

Online Videos

The citation for a film downloaded from the Web should include all the information provided for other film formats plus the medium "Web," Web site information, and date of access. Online sources are so varied that you will not always find an exact example for a source you wish to cite, however, and you might need to improvise in some instances. An online video released only on the Web could be cited as follows (note that we add the supplementary information "Flash animation" at the end of the citation even though there is no specific MLA format for such a source):

> "Time for Some Campaignin'." Dir. Gregg Spiridellis and Evan Spiridellis. JibJab Media, July 2008.
> Web. 5 Sept. 2008. Flash animation.

Online Images

Some online images come from print publications. In such cases, you should treat the citation like a print source online—giving the original publication data plus the media, date, database (if any), and date of access. If the image is found online with no attributed print publication, you can treat it like a Web-only source.

> "Newton's Reflector Telescope." N.d. Courtesy of the Royal Astronomical Society. *Amazing Space:*
> *History of the Telescope.* Web. 27 Jan. 2009.

Academic Web Sources

Many instructors maintain scholarly Web sites to provide their students with useful information for entering into the academic discussion surrounding a particular subject. These sites can be very helpful for a student who is beginning to research a topic, and they tend to be reliable because they are generally written and updated by professionals in the field. They range in scope, purpose, and quality but can prove helpful as introductory sources. When a Web site lists no author, compiler, or editor, begin with the site's title, as you would with a print source lacking a listed author.

> Campbell, Donna. "Frank Norris." *Naturalism in American Literature.* Washington State U, July
> 2005. Web. 18 Aug. 2005.
>
> London, Joan Griffith. "A Short Biography of Jack London." *The Jack London Online Collection.*
> Sonoma State U, 25 July 2006. Web. 8 Sept. 2008.

Print Publications on the Web

In addition to the standard information for a printed source, give the name of the service (such as *ProQuest, Academic Search Premier, LexisNexis, JSTOR*) through which you accessed the source as well as the medium and the date you accessed it. The following example is for a scholarly journal—the initial information remains the same as in the print version. Sometimes page numbers disappear in online reproductions, in which case you will use "n. pag." to indicate that no page numbers are given.

> Orkin, Martin. "Remaking Shakespeare: Performance across Media, Genres, and Culture."
> *Shakespeare Quarterly* 55.6 (2004): 488-92. *ProQuest.* Web. 5 Aug. 2007.
>
> Stephen, Andrew. "The Poisonous Legacy of 9/11." *New Statesman* 24 June 2007: 24-26. *EBSCO.*
> Web. 20 July 2007.

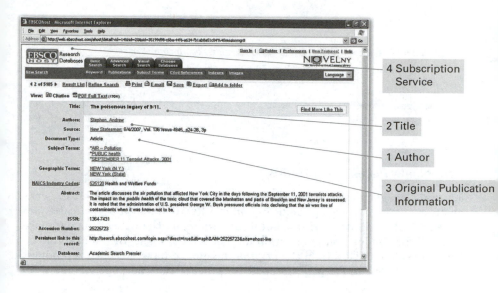

Stephen, Andrew. "The Poisonous Legacy of 9/11." *New Statesman*. 4 June

2007: 24-26. *Academic Search Premier*. EBSCO. New York Public Library.

20 June 2007. <http://www.epnet.com>.

Online Books

Fitzgerald, F. Scott. *The Great Gatsby*. 1925. N. pag. *Project Gutenberg Australia*. Web. 10 Sept. 2008.

CD-ROMs

Citing CD-ROMs is much like citing books and periodicals—the primary distinction between the two types of CD-ROM is whether they are single issues or published periodically. You may also find data on diskettes or magnetic tape (label them as such if you do), but the CD-ROM is currently the favored medium.

Nonperiodically Published CD-ROMs

Citations for CD-ROMs are similar to those of their print counterparts, but they sometimes have supplementary information, as in the Troy example below, where there is a different publisher for the disc than for the original source.

"Pretend." *The Oxford English Dictionary*. 2nd ed. Oxford: Oxford UP, 1992. CD-ROM.

Troy, Leo. "Ship and Boat Building." *Almanac of Business and Industrial Financial Ratios* 34 (2003): 157-58. Chart. CD-ROM. Aspen Publishing. 2003.

Note: Supplementary information comes after the medium, "CD-ROM" in this instance.

Periodically Published CD-ROMs

Journals, magazines, and newspapers sometimes publish reference works, abstracts, or back issues periodically on CD-ROMs. Treat a periodically published CD-ROM like its print counterpart; then add the title of the database, name of the vendor, and publication date of the database. In the example below, the page numbers from the original magazine have not been reproduced in the CD-ROM, so "n. pag." is used to indicate that no page numbers are available.

McNamara, Tom. "How I Survive in the City." *Mother Earth News* May-June 1970: n. pag. CD-ROM. *Mother Earth News the First Ten Years*. Ogden Publications. 2003.

Winging It: How to Cite Unusual Sources

If a source has useful information, it can be a valid resource, and it can be cited. If you come across an unusual source for which you cannot find a citation model, you can still effectively cite it. Keep in mind the basic formula—Author, Title, Publisher/Publication, Date, and Medium—and make a list of the information available from your source. Be sure to assign the source a working title (or functional description) when none is established. For example, The Republic of Tea Company prints a chart of the caffeine content (per 5-ounce measure) of coffee, black tea, oolong tea, and green tea on its tea tins. Our second unusual source is a Scottish board game. Our final offbeat source is a list of safety rules for vacuum cleaner operation as set forth in an owner's manual. Here's how we would cite them:

"Caffeine Content." Novato: The Republic of Tea Co., 2004. Tea Tin.

Duncan, Alexander. *Enigma: A Game of Riddles*. Edinburgh: Drumond Park, 1988. Board Game.

"Important Safeguards." *Eureka Lightweight Upright Vacuum Cleaner Owner's Guide*. Bloomington: Eureka, 2001. Print.

Credits

Cover, title page, copyright page, and p. 99 from Freakonomics by Steven D. Levitt and Stephen J. Dubner Copyright (c) 2005 by Steven D. Levitt and Stephen J. Dubner Reprinted by permission of HarperCollins Publishers.

Screen capture of "The Poisonous Legacy of 9/11" from EBSCO website, www.ebsco.com. Reprinted (or reproduced if electronic permission) by permission of EBSCO Publishing.

"Texts and Other Symbolic Spaces" by Jens Brockmeier, *Mind, Culture, and Activity*, January 2001, 8, (3), 215–231, reprinted by permission of Taylor & Francis Group, www.informaworld.com.

Index